Echoes of
GEORGIA
FOOTBALL

Echoes of
GEORGIA
FOOTBALL

The Greatest Stories Ever Told

Edited by Ken Samelson

TRIUMPH
B O O K S
CHICAGO

Library of Congress Cataloging-in-Publication Data

Echoes of Georgia football : the greatest stories ever told / edited by Ken Samelson.
    p. cm.
Includes bibliographical references.
ISBN-13: 978-1-57243-875-0 (alk. paper)
ISBN-10: 1-57243-875-4 (alk. paper)
    1. University of Georgia—Football—History. 2. Georgia Bulldogs (Football team)—History. 3. Football players—Georgia—History. I. Samelson, Ken.

GV958.G44.E24 2006
796.332'630975818—dc22

2006014326

This book is available in quantity at special discounts for your group or organization. For further information, contact:

Triumph Books
542 South Dearborn Street
Suite 750
Chicago, Illinois 60605
(312) 939-3330
Fax (312) 663-3557

Printed in U.S.A.
ISBN-13: 978-1-57243-875-0
ISBN-10: 1-57243-875-4
Design by Patricia Frey
Photos courtesy of AP/Wide World Photos

CONTENTS

FOREWORD

Most people know that I became a Georgia Bulldog when the university hired me on December 4, 1963, as the head football coach, but few people know that my relationship with the Bulldogs actually goes back more than 60 years. I scouted the Bulldogs for eight years as an Auburn assistant coach, and I never missed the Georgia-Florida game in Jacksonville. And, of course, I played against Georgia several times as a player at Auburn.

Even growing up as a young boy in Mobile, Alabama, one of my hobbies was clipping out newspaper articles about my favorite teams and players and gluing them into my sports scrapbook (which I still have, by the way). Although I have several Bulldog All-Americans in my scrapbook, the two most notable are Frank Sinkwich and Charley Trippi—two of Georgia's most legendary players.

So my history with Georgia goes back a long way, which gives me great insight into some of the Bulldogs' greatest teams, players, and moments. I participated, for instance, in the dedication ceremony for a historical marker on the site of Georgia's first football game—Herty Field—up on North Campus. I was part of the 1992 centennial celebration of our first football game against Auburn, which was held in Piedmont Park in Atlanta in 1892. And during my time at Georgia we celebrated the 50th and 75th anniversaries of Sanford Stadium. I saw the stadium grow from a capacity of 43,621 when I arrived in 1964 to 92,746 plus 77 SkySuites when I retired in 2005.

I've been fortunate to have developed friendships with many of the legendary figures in Georgia football history. When I became head coach, one of my first decisions was to go see Hall of Fame coach Wally Butts to pay my respects. Coach Butts always appreciated that gesture, and he wrote to me after each game, to either congratulate me or to offer encouragement. I first met Sinkwich over lunch at the Dairy Queen on Broad Street in Athens shortly after I came to Georgia, and I was in awe. Trippi still lives in Athens, and we have been longtime friends. Fran Tarkenton has been one of our greatest supporters since arriving in Athens and still follows our football fortunes closely.

I also became friends with the charming and beloved Vernon "Catfish" Smith, one of Georgia's first Hall of Famers. And let's not forget the incomparable radio voice of the Dawgs, Larry "Run, Lindsay,

Run" Munson, with whom I've shared fishing trips and football stories for 40 years. Munson arrived in my third year as a Bulldog, replacing the beloved Ed Thilenius, who called Georgia games for decades with the colorful Bill Munday. It was Munday who coined the famous saying, "I was a Bulldog born and Bulldog bred. And when I die I will be a Bulldog dead."

When I first came to Georgia, I met and got to know the successful coach of the late 1920s and 1930s, Harry Mehre, who by then was an entertaining, witty football analyst and writer. After I came to Georgia, I saw him often when he was on the speaking circuit, and he always reminded me to enjoy "the honeymoon," as he called the time period before coaching my first game. He left Georgia for Ole Miss and a lucrative "lifetime contract." A few years later, Mehre often said, they declared him "legally dead" and fired him. Mehre was the Georgia coach when Sanford Stadium was dedicated in 1929 and when Catfish Smith scored all 15 points that led the Bulldogs to upset Yale, a power-house at the time. That day was also the birth of the famous hedges that still surround the playing field. As a coach, I especially enjoyed getting the opposition "between the hedges."

But the greatest Bulldogs of all, coaches Dan Magill and Bill Hartman, were my constant historical resources and taught me more about the traditions and spirit of the Dawgs than anyone else. "What-a-Ya-Got Loran" Smith, who idolizes Magill and Hartman, has been a friend since my first day as a Bulldog, and he has carried on the tradition of providing a new wave of Bulldogs folklore.

And how could any history of the Georgia Bulldogs be complete without our beloved mascot, the greatest mascot in America? The Seiler family of Savannah—Sonny, Cecelia, and the kids—started and has continued the line of mascots, watching over them for half a century. I've served with them all.

Of course, I've been fortunate to have also coached some of Georgia's legendary players, some of whom are already members of the College Football Hall of Fame—Outland Trophy–winner Bill Stanfill, defensive back Terry Hoage, tailback and Heisman Trophy–winner Herschel Walker, and kicker Kevin Butler. Who can forget Butler's 60-yard kick to beat Clemson in 1984? And we've had our share of great teams that have earned distinction: the SEC champions from 1966, 1968, and 1976 and the run in the early 1980s that produced the national champions of 1980; the SEC champions in 1980, 1981, and 1982; and the great Cotton Bowl champions of 1983. The group of players from the 1980s produced a 43–4–1 record, best in the nation during that four-year period. And who will ever forget the Wonder Dawgs of '78 and the Junkyard Dawgs of '75, a group inspired by defensive coordinator Erk Russell?

I am especially proud that one of my last major decisions as athletics director was to hire Mark Richt, who has given us championship teams and a stable program that is a model of integrity around the country. He has been responsible for some great teams and players who have given our fans thrilling moments.

You'll find words about many of these teams, players, and coaches and much more in the stories that make up this unique collection. They represent what Georgia football is all about and bring to these pages some of the color, passion, and history of the program for all to read.

—Vince Dooley
Former head football coach
University of Georgia

Echoes of
GEORGIA
FOOTBALL

Head coach Vince Dooley is carried off the field in celebration of Georgia football's finest moment to date, the Bulldogs' 17–10 victory over Notre Dame in the Sugar Bowl on January 1, 1981, to claim the national championship.

Section I
THE GAMES

Atlanta Constitution

SPORTS OF WINTER

Did you know that the Bulldogs' very first game was played in the dead of winter? On January 30, 1892, they took on Mercer's team at Herty Field. The details were in the next day's Atlanta Constitution.

The winter winds of '92 are fanning new life into the athletic world of the South. Southern athletes are leaping at last into the happy realization that there is as good muscle below the belt of Mason and Dixon's line as there is above it. [The prediction is] that southward all eyes will be turned within the next few seasons to see records on the field, track, and diamond break to pieces and tumble to a depth known only to McGinty, since his rash and world-recorded leap to the bottom of the sea, and parts unknown generally. [Refers to a popular song from 1889, "Down Went McGinty," about a man who fell into the sea, never to be heard from again.]

Why should the grass on the campus of a southern college grow rank to weed, unmolested by the obtruding foot of some sturdy athletes? Why should the invigorating, health-giving, breezy sports of winter flush the cheek of the northern student with rosy bloom, while the southern youth at college languishes in indolence and bad health, unfit for study, lazy, and almost tired of life?

This thing has been kept up too long already, and the southern colleges are coming to the realization in a hurry that something must be done to develop body as well as mind.

It is not necessary; it is not wise to run wild with enthusiasm in this line of reform. That would lead to the neglect of study for athletic sports and games. But it is necessary, and it is wise to go about physical culture in moderation, and the colleges of the South are to be commended for just such a spirit which seems to be sweeping over every campus this season.

The exciting game of football between the university and Mercer University, played on the Athens grounds yesterday, starts the championship games between Georgia colleges, and the promise is given that this will be kept up at a lively rate the remainder of the winter and spring terms.

There is an abundance of good athletic material among the Georgia colleges and, in fact, all over the southern states. The truth is that many of the strongest football teams and baseball teams of northern colleges draw their strongest pillars from southern youths attending those colleges.

Of course, colleges like the University of Georgia or Mercer University cannot get together as clever a lot of football players this year as many of the northern colleges because they have not as large a body of students to select from as do those colleges at the North, but they were good teams, nevertheless, that met on the fields in Athens yesterday, and a good game resulted.

The University Colors Wave Triumphantly over Mercer

The red and crimson of the University of Georgia waves triumphantly, and a score of 50 to nothing shows the university boys know how to play football. It was the first match game between colleges ever played this far south, and naturally an interest was aroused in it.

The Mercer team arrived at 12:00 in two special cars and were accompanied by fully 200 students and citizens. They were taken in charge by the university boys and made to feel at home. Long before 3:00 the crowd began to assemble, and by the time the game was called, nearly 1,500 people were on the ground.

The Lucy Cobb girls and Home School girls were all present with university colors upon them, and the two goals were decorated beautifully, one in yellow and black, the colors of Mercer, and the other in black and crimson, the colors of the university.

At 3:00 the boys raised the college yell, "Rah, rah, rah, ta Georgia!" followed by Mercer with a "Rah, rah, rah, U-ni-v-sis-boom ah Versisty, Mercer." The teams took their position, and umpire Frank Lupton of Auburn and referee Ike Cabaniss of Macon called the game.

Excitement Ran High

Interest was at a high pitch when Mercer kicked off the ball, and then all was excitement.

On the first pass back Mercer lost three yards and made no gain on the second.

George Shackelford lost two yards, then Charles Herty grabbed the ball and, making an extraordinary run, touched down behind the goal. Score: 4 to nothing.

Mercer again has the ball and punts it. John Kimball secures it and makes a good run. In the scuffle E. W. Frey secured it, ran several yards, passed to Henry Brown, then to Herty, then to Kimball. After a great deal of scuffling, Kimball made a good run and touched down. Score: 8 to nothing.

The next touchdown was made quickly by Herty assisted by Brown. Brown kicked a goal; score: 14–0.

The next tilt was furious and ended by a long kick of 65 yards by Brown, caught by a Mercer man, who in turn was caught by Shackelford and carried over the line for a safety, bringing the score to 16–0.

Then came an exciting part, when the two teams remained at the 10-yard line for quite a while, making brilliant plays.

Pretty Work, This

By a splendid piece of headwork Herty passes to Kimball, who makes one of the prettiest runs of the game and rams the fourth touchdown; score: 20–0. A goal was then kicked by Brown, which ran up the score 22–0. Brown in the next part made a splendid run to the 10-yard line, and Herty made a touchdown. Brown kicked a goal, and the first half ended with a score of 28–0 in favor of the university. In the second half Brown carried the ball to the 8-yard line by a splendid run, but foul was claimed. Then Shackelford, by several good plays, made advantage for the university. Brown made a run of 67 yards amidst terrific cheering, and Herty touched down. Score: 32–0.

In the next sport Herty carried the ball to the 5-yard line, but Mercer put it back to the 25-yard line. Kimball made a star play through the crowd and touched down.

Brown kicked a goal. Score: 38–0.

After the ball next left the center, Shackelford advanced it 20 yards, and Herty touched down. Score: 42–0.

Sprained His Ankle

Offerman, of Mercer, sprained his ankle, and Emmett Small took his place. Small made a good advance, when Shackelford, grabbing the ball, eluded the entire team and ran through the goal and touched down. Score: 46–0.

The last struggle was a manful one on both sides, when Brown and Herty scored the last touchdown, making the score 50–0.

The crowd was wild. Hats flew into the air, and the boys were hoisted on the shoulders of the crowd and borne around in triumph.

The Mercer team took their defeat most gracefully, for they were a fine set of boys. The university will play Auburn in Atlanta on the 20th of February.

The Athens Men

The average weight of the men Athens put against Mercer: 157 pounds.

The average weight of her men on the rush line is 167 pounds.

A word or two about the men who wrestled with Mercer in the game will be of interest, especially since another game is soon to be played by those men right here in Atlanta on the 20th of next month with the team from Auburn, Alabama.

Mr. E. W. Frey, of Marietta, Georgia, the largest man in college, holds down the position of center rush on the team. Frey weighs 202 pounds and stands 6'1" in his football shoes. He is a senior this year, and a man with a cool head and the best of natures. He has done some good practice work with the team and gives any opponent who may come in contact with him a sharp tussle.

The tallest man on the team, and, by the way, one of the most agile players and best runners in college, is Park Howell, the right guard. He stands 6'2" in his stockings, weighs 165 pounds, and has the best running record of any man at the university.

Mr. George Shackelford, of Jefferson, Georgia, is the left guard. He entered college last September, but since that time has made a splendid reputation as an athlete and, in fact, is engaged in most all of the prominent field sports. He is 6' in height, with a weight of 175 pounds.

As right tackle the team will place Mr. A. O. Halsey, who made such a wide reputation last season as the best all-round baseball player in college. He is from Charleston, and since coming to Georgia has made it lively for the Georgia boys in the classroom. His height is 6', and he weighs 165 pounds.

Mr. R. B. Nalley, the famous catcher of last year's baseball team, is the left tackle. He is well built and very hard to pass on a run with the ball: height, 5'11"; weight, 170.

Manager Lane, from Macon, enjoys quite a wide athletic reputation, especially in the gymnasium. He is a member of the senior engineering class and since entering college has been a prime mover in most of the athletic work of any moment. With a weight of 135 pounds, and height 5'7", he has been favorably placed as right end of the team. His solid build makes him a strong man for that position.

Mr. L. D. Fricks, of the sophomore class, holds down the left end for the team. He is fully capable to take care of his position, as is shown by his work in other athletic sports. Height, 6'; weight, 100 pounds.

As far as athletic reputation is concerned, no man has enjoyed more of it since entering college than Billy Gramling, another South Carolinian. Billy came up from Charleston in 1889, since which time he has been among the leaders in the classroom as well as in the athletic field. His height is 5'7", and weight 135. It is not his dimensions which enable him to hold down so well his position of quarterback, but his natural strength and activity.

Captain Frank Herty, of the team, boasts the reputation of the best ball pitcher in the college, having been pitcher of the college team last year. He is small, being 5'6" in height and weighing 125 pounds, but that by no means interferes with his good qualities as a football player.

In fact, he holds down to advantage one of the most important positions on the team, being right halfback.

Mr. John Kimball, of Atlanta, has been employed as left halfback. Since entering the law class last September, he has taken an active part in athletic sports. He graduated a year ago from the military college at Auburn, Alabama, where he had quite a reputation as a ballplayer as well as in other lines. His height is but 5'6", but he is built solidly and weighs 145 pounds.

The fullback, and a good one he is, too, is Mr. Henry O. Brown, from Augusta. He has been at Athens but a few months, but has been a prime mover in football and other sports. He is one of the best all-around football players in college. His height is 5'7½", with a weight of 145 pounds.

The club feels quite seriously the loss of one of its best and most active players, who was to have been one of the halfbacks. He is Mr. W. B. Armstrong, who, in a practice game the other day, broke one of the bones in his leg just above the ankle. He will be unable to walk on it for a month to come. This unfortunate accident would, it was thought, somewhat handicap the club, but his position was well filled by Mr. John Kimball, of Atlanta.

Yesterday was the first time the boys played a championship game, but it was done in great shape, and they kept it lively for the spectators and for the Mercer boys as well.

Mercer's Kickers

Mercer's team is itself "no slouch," to use language familiar in the gym.

Her men average well in weight, in size, and age, and they are very well selected, too. They are active enough on the field, and not infrequently do they catch the approving and stirring applause of the crowds around the field.

The general make-up of the team is shown on the trainer's book as follows:

	Weight	Height	Age	County
Nash	155	5'10"	17	Lincoln
Napier	160	6'	19	Walker
Atkinson	175	6'	17	Butts
Madden	118	5'5"	17	Glynn
Offerman	145	5'7"	17	Pierce
Chapman	200	5'11"	22	Liberty
Brown	195	6'1"	21	Hart
C. Peteet	150	5'11"	18	Morgan
Anderson	185	5'9"	18	Chambers (Alabama)
Turpin	146	5'11"	18	Bibb
Beggs	148	5'9"	19	Bibb

	Weight	Height	Age	County
Small	150	6'	16	Bibb
D. Peteet	148	5'9"	17	Morgan
Conner	148	5'11"	18	Bibb
Brown	170	6'	17	Bibb

The places taken by the men of the team are as follows: W. M. Conner, one of the best athletes at Mercer and a famous kicker, is sub-end rush; Reed Nash, a muscular athlete, right-end rush; Captain Dave Boggs, fullback; R. E. Anderson, right guard; P. V. Brown, sub-center rush; J. V. Brown, center rush; Chapman, left guard; Walter Turpin, right halfback; Napier, left tackle; Morris Madden, quarterback; C. P. Atkinson, right tackle; Denny Peteet, sub halfback; Offerman, left half-back; Cland Peteet, left-end rush; Emmett Small, sub halfback.

Mercer has an all-round good team and is destined yet to make a fine showing among the championship games of southern college teams. They have good grounds upon which to play, and that counts for much. With just a little more training the boys will, indeed, make a crack team in every sense of that term.

Some exciting championship games may be expected among the Georgia colleges. Oxford ought to be holding up her head, too, in this line, and when she does there will be a triangular shape to the fun. Oxford's forte seems to be baseball, however, and maybe it is this that she is waiting in which to play the winning hand.

Robert F. Kelley, *The New York Times*

YALE BEATEN, 15–0, BY GEORGIA 11 IN A STIRRING GAME

The very first game in Sanford Stadium was a historic one, a shutout of eastern power Yale in which Vernon "Catfish" Smith made a name for himself by scoring all 15 points. The New York Times' *account of the contest follows.*

Yale's first football visit to the South ended in disaster on a summer-like afternoon today, as 35,000 persons, some of them in their shirt-sleeves, watched the University of Georgia topple the Blue completely and convincingly by the margin of 15–0.

A blocked kick on Yale's goal line in the second period and the recovery of it for a touchdown by Vernon Smith, Georgia's left end; a safety after a mixed Yale signal in the third period; and a long twisting pass to the same Smith with a following 12-yard run in the fourth period tell the story of the scoring.

But those details fail utterly to tell the story of the hard and decisive tackling that broke the men of Yale this afternoon. Smith kicked the goal after the first score and missed the second, but none of the thousands of southerners minded that. The end came a few minutes later with the roaring crowd descending on the field to celebrate Georgia's great victory.

Some Arrive by Plane

The victory put the crowning touch to a perfect day for southern football. The biggest crowd this little town ever has held for a game came by special train, airplane, and thousands of cars; they saw the ceremonious dedication of the new Sanford Stadium. Then they settled back for the contest in a setting more like baseball than football. The temperature was well over 70 degrees, and the sun was hot.

There is no doubt that Yale suffered badly from the heat. The Blue used so many substitutes it was impossible for the scorer to keep track of them, sending them in at times in groups of five or six. But it also was true that Georgia was much the better team today.

The Yale attack was stopped dead in its tracks for the most part by the hard charging of the Georgia forwards, and of 13 Yale passes, six were incomplete and two were intercepted.

Albie Booth, the little quarterback, entered the game halfway in the second period and played into the last period, but Yale never was able to shake him free for a twisting run, and only in spots did he turn in the sensational carrying he showed against Vermont in the Bowl.

Leads in First Downs

On the other hand, Yale did pretty well with Georgia's attack, the southerners gaining six first downs to Yale's seven, but the winners were by far the more alert team and took quick and decisive advantage of the breaks, played smarter football throughout, and clearly earned their victory.

Yale kicked off, and play stayed pretty well in Georgia's territory during the first period, but never with a Yale attack threatening. It was Yale's punting that kept it there as the teams exchanged kicks.

Yale, at the start, was rushing Smith, who also did his team's punting, and hurrying him. Then came the first break when a low, bounding punt got away from Wilson, and [John] Davidson recovered for Georgia on Yale's 46-yard line. Yale held and forced a kick over the line, but play had been shifted to Yale's half of the field.

After an exchange of punts in the second period, things broke suddenly for Georgia. [Armin] Waugh came back well with a Yale punt that followed a long one by Smith to Yale's 35-yard line, a run of 12 yards. Yale braced strongly, but [Weddington] Kelley, Georgia's other end, made an amazing catch of a forward with two Yale men in front of him on the 20-yard line for a first down there. Then Waugh shot wide around left end to the 8-yard line.

Gallant Stand in Vain

Yale made a gallant stand with Loeser jamming through and Hikok following him a play or so later to throw men for losses. Yale took the ball on downs on her 7-yard line, but the next play saw the turning of the scales. The Yale line, weakened by its desperate stand, let Georgia sift through. A knot of southerners blocked McClennan's punt, and Smith fell on the ball for the first touchdown.

Yale came back with one of its few real stretches of running. Booth showing well on one run of 18 yards. But it was stopped on Georgia's 30-yard line, and Booth tried a drop from the 38-yard line that fell far short of the mark for a touchback.

It wasn't far into the third period when Smith's line punting brought another score. He placed one out of bounds on Yale's

12-yard line and on the next play came the safety. Apparently signals were mixed, for Booth was not near the center's pass, which rolled over the goal line. He picked it up but couldn't get back across the goal line.

[Jack] Roberts came back well with the free kick that followed, and play started pretty much in Yale territory for the rest of the period. Georgia had the ball on Yale's 35-yard line at the start of the final period but lost it when an incomplete pass came on the fourth down— Booth batted the ball down.

There followed soon after the first real chance Yale had. Booth sent away a fine punt, and when [Austin] Downs fumbled on his 30-yard line Captain Greene of Yale snatched the ball and, forgetting the new fumble rule, raced on across the goal. He was called back to the 30-yard line. [All fumbles ruled dead at point of recovery.]

Then Booth shot through his right tackle on a pretty run to the 14-yard line. Plunges carried it to the 6, but Georgia's line rose and smothered Yale's last effort and took away the ball.

Yale seemed on the way back with a forward pass that carried inside the 20-yard line, but Smith once more rose to the occasion and intercepted a lateral pass. He punted out, and a few plays later [Bennie] Rothstein intercepted a forward at midfield and carried it to the Yale 45-yard line.

Georgia was forced to punt again, but later gained the ball on an intercepted pass, this time on the 30-yard line. From there, after two short plunges, [Spurgeon] Chandler shot a long pass to Smith, who made a running catch on the 13-yard line and continued on unmolested for the final score of the day.

The lineup:

Game Summary

Georgia (15)		Yale (0)
V. Smith	LE	Hikok
Rose	LH	Marting
Mattax	LG	Loeser
Boland	C	Palmer
Leathers	RG	Greene
Frishee	RT	Vincent
Kelley	RE	Walker
Downs	QB	Wilson
Dickens	LH	Snead
Davidson	RH	Miller
Rothstein	FB	Dunn

Score by Quarters

Georgia	0	7	2	6	15
Yale	0	0	0	0	0

Touchdowns—V. Smith (2). Point after touchdown—V. Smith (drop kick). Safety—Georgia.

Substitutions—Georgia: Waugh for Dickens, Roberts for Rothstein, Tassapoulous for Boland, Dickens for Waugh, Chandler for Davidson, Rothstein for Roberts, Maffett for Kelley, Bryant for Rose. Yale: McClennan for Snead, Hare for Loeser, Booth for Wilson, Taylor for McClennan, Austen for Dunn, Cruikshant for Miller, Austen for Dunn, Barres for Walker, Hall for Marting, Lincham for Greene, Hall for Booth, Gwyn for Palmer, Lindenberg for Taylor.

Referee—Ed Thorp, De La Salle. Umpire—J. P. Major, Auburn. Field judge—Hutchens, Purdue. Linesman—Black, Davidson. Time of periods—15 minutes.

Louis Effrat, *The New York Times*

GEORGIA DEFEATS TEXAS CHRISTIAN

Another first—Georgia made its initial bowl appearance a successful one with a decisive rout of TCU in the 1942 Orange Bowl. The victory capped a 9–1–1 record under Wally Butts and was the precursor to the 1942 national championship season. Here is The New York Times' *account of this game from January 2, 1942.*

With Frankie Sinkwich, Georgia's All-American back who is often referred to as the "Cracked-Jaw Cracker," pacing the attack with a brilliant performance, the Bulldogs from Athens conquered Texas Christian University's Horned Frogs before a crowd of 35,505 shirt-sleeved fans in the eighth-annual Orange Bowl classic today.

The score of this free-scoring, picturesque encounter staged in a setting of orange pageantry that pleased the eye, was 40–26. Such a count indicates an overabundance of action, with never a dull moment.

This, however, is not entirely true. There were moments of disinterest brought on by the ineffectiveness of TCU throughout the opening half, which terminated with the Bulldogs out in front by a 33–7 margin, which soared to 40–7 in the third period.

Gillespie Hits Stride

Then the Horned Frogs shook off their lethargic tactics, sloppy tackling, and faulty blocking and suddenly came out of it with a determination to save themselves from an utter rout. Kyle Gillespie, hampered by the inability of his mates to help him earlier, hit his true stride. Emery Nix also came through with a few sparkling plays, and the general improvement in the Texans was obvious.

The Frogs struck for one tally in the third session and two touchdowns in the final quarter, and even if it was too late for them to pull the game out of the fire, they wound up the afternoon with a creditable showing.

But this was definitely Sinkwich's show. He ran and passed Georgia to a merited victory, inspired his mates to greater accomplishments, and left no doubt as to his football prowess. Three of his passes brought as many touchdowns, and once he dashed 43 yards on his own for another tally. Truly, the sight of this heavily helmeted junior, whose fractured jaw still requires special protection, personally out-gaining the entire TCU squad will long be remembered by the crowd which saw it today.

From the very outset it appeared that on this given day the Horned Frogs would be no match for the Bulldogs. Even while the Texans were in possession, the feeling was that Georgia was the superior outfit. Precisely how superior [was] the only question that remained as early as the first period. Not for an instant could one see a ray of hope for Texas Christian, not even when Dutch Meyer's 11 gained a 7–6 edge midway in the opening quarter.

Pass Defense Weak

And as the struggle proceeded, the impression was that TCU at its very best would have tough sledding against Georgia as it was today.

In the matter of pass defense the Texans ran around in circles as though they had never heard of such a thing. Gillespie was given less protection than a reckless driver, and so his reputation along with his team's suffered tremendously.

Of course, it may have been that the red-hot Bulldogs—who, unlike their unimaginative opponents, seldom made a wrong move—had a lot to do with the way this battle went. If Georgia had no one else on the gridiron, which isn't exactly true, Sinkwich was there, and Sinkwich, himself, was as much a one-man gang as Ace Parker, Sid Luckman, and other football greats ever were. From a Texas viewpoint, it's good that this All-American did not play a full game. He was in and out all after-noon, otherwise it might have developed into a gridiron travesty.

Sinkwich was truly magnificent, but he did have help. Cliff Kimsey, a fine blocker, did his share, as did Lamar Davis, Ken Keuper, and Andy Dudish in the backfield. Up front [Thomas] Greene, [Greene] Keltner, Harry Kuniansky, and Walter Ruark were outstanding. For TCU, Derrell Palmer came through with a number of nice defensive plays.

Touchdown in Five Minutes

Just about five minutes after the start, Georgia moved quickly and unfalteringly to its initial touchdown, a 66-yard advance that required just seven plays. Keuper went over from the 1-yard line for the score.

A fumble by Davis, recovered by Bill Crawford on the 19, led to the first Texas tally, with Gillespie plunging over from the 4. Frank Medanich converted the extra point from placement and sent TCU ahead, 7–6, but not for long. A minute and a half later Sinkwich tossed a perfect aerial to Mel Conger, who sidestepped every would-be tackler and scored easily. The play covered 61 yards.

In the same period Sinkwich passed to Kimsey in a 60-yard touchdown maneuver, and Leo Costa succeeded with his kick.

Throughout the next period Georgia was completely in control and tallied two more touchdowns. A 15-yard aerial from Sinkwich to Keuper brought one and a 23-yard heave from Jim Todd to Davis the other. Each time Costa converted.

Early in the third, Sinkwich, seeking a receiver but finding none, split the middle and traveled 43 yards for the prettiest touchdown of the day. Costa made the count 40–7. At this point the Bulldogs relaxed long enough for the Horned Frogs to score 19 points. All were the results of passes, Nix and Gillespie tossing 20- and 15-yard end-zone aerials to Bruce Alford and Gillespie completing a 53-yard overhead thrust.

Orange Bowl Lineup

Georgia 40		TCU 26
Poschner	LE	Alford
Greene	LT	Palmer
Ruark	LG	Crawford
Godwin	C	Woodnin
Kuniansky	RG	Pugh
Keltner	RT	Adams
V. Davis	RE	Roach
Kimsey	QB	Gillespie
Sinkwich	LH	Sparks
L. Davis	RH	Medanich
Keuper	FB	Kring

Score by Periods

Georgia	19	14	7	0	40
TCU	7	0	7	12	26

Touchdowns—Keuper 2, Conger, Sinkwich, Kimsey, L. Davis, Gillespie, Alford 2, Kring. Points after touchdowns—Costa 4, Medanich 2.

Substitutes

Georgia—Ends: Conger, Phelps. Tackles: Lewis, Ellenson, Posey. Guards: Burt, Miller. Center: Costa. Backs: Dudish, Bray, Todd.

Texas Christian—Ends: Brumbaugh, Slover. Tackles: Hampton, Flowers. Guards: Harter, Moss, Rogers. Center: Blackstone. Backs: Conway, Ramsey, Vanhall, Taylor, Montgomery, Bagley, Nix, Bierman.

Referee—John J. Lynch, Holy Cross. Umpire—Roscoe Minton, Philadelphia. Linesman—D. Jackson, Emory and Henry. Field judge—Charles Y. Swartz, Rice. Time of periods—15 minutes.

Statistics of the Game

	Georgia	TCU
First downs	12	8
Yards gained rushing	188	101
Forward passes	23	23
Forwards completed	12	9
Yards gained, forwards	288	176
Forwards intercepted by	6	4
Number of punts	4	7
*Average distance		
of punts, yards	44	43
Fumbles	3	0
Own fumbles recovered	0	0
Penalties	5	3
Yards lost, penalties	45	25

*From point where ball was kicked

Gene Asher, *Georgia Trend* magazine

THE MAN WHO BROKE THE DROUGHT

Going into the 1957 matchup with archrival Georgia Tech, the Bulldogs had dropped eight consecutive games in the series. It took a heroic effort by Theron Sapp to put an end to the streak. Gene Asher told the story in this article from March 2003.

With a single touchdown, Theron Sapp did as much for Georgia pride as anyone in Bulldogs history.

November 30, 1957, was a subfreezing but delightful afternoon for Bulldogs fans at Grant Field. A stiff wind was blowing out of the northeast as some 40,000 fans—mostly Tech partisans—came to see if Tech could make it nine consecutive victories over Georgia or if the Dawgs would find a way to break the drought. They did, thanks to Theron Coleman Sapp, a mighty fullback out of Lanier High School in Macon, Georgia.

The Bulldogs were suffering through a third-consecutive losing season and had not scored a touchdown against Tech in four long years. But this was another day. After a scoreless first half, Sapp recovered a fumble at midfield. On third-and-12 at the Tech 39, quarterback Charlie Britt hit Jimmy Orr with a 13-yard pass for a first down at the Tech 26. From then on it was all Sapp...Sapp...Sapp.

He crashed into the Tech forewall on six consecutive plays, down to the Tech 1-yard line. On fourth down Britt again handed off to Sapp, who powered his way into the right side of the Tech line for the Dogs' first touchdown against Tech since 1953 and the only touchdown of the game. Ken Cooper converted the extra point, giving Georgia a 7–0 victory. Sapp crossed the goal line only six times in his Georgia career, but he did as much for Georgia pride with one touchdown as anyone in Bulldogs history, including Frankie Sinkwich, Charley Trippi, and Herschel Walker.

The late, legendary Georgia Tech coach Bobby Dodd said of Sapp, "Walker won the national championship for Georgia [1980] and was awarded the Heisman Trophy [1982], but to older Bulldogs who suffered through the 1950s, Sapp's breaking the drought was greater. He silenced eight years of bragging from Tech students and alumni. Breaking the drought was a remarkable achievement."

Sapp's No. 40 was retired two months after the 1958 Tech game. His jersey, along with Sinkwich's, Trippi's, and Walker's, hangs in the lobby of the Butts-Mehre Building at the University of Georgia. Sinkwich gained 2,271 yards and scored 30 touchdowns, Trippi 1,669 yards and 32 touchdowns, and Walker 5,259 yards and 52 touchdowns. Sapp rushed for just 1,269 yards, but he ripped the Jackets line to shreds in breaking the drought.

Says the drought breaker, "I never dreamed my jersey would be retired."

Sapp was named to All-Southeastern Conference teams in 1957 and 1958. He led the Bulldogs to a second win over Tech in 1958, 16–3. He was named most valuable player in the Tech game in 1957 and 1958.

Sapp was named Georgia's Back of the Decade (1950–1959). His late coach, Wally Butts, called him "the best offensive fullback I ever had." Sapp went to Georgia with a broken neck and finished an eight-season professional football career with a broken leg. In between, he was captain of the 1958 Bulldogs, named Most Valuable Player in the North-South and Blue-Gray College All-Star Games, and helped lead the Philadelphia Eagles to an NFL championship.

Today, the 67-year-old Sapp lives with his wife of 37 years, Kay, in a two-story, five-bedroom house on 12 acres in Evans, Georgia, about 15 miles north of Augusta. At 6'0", he weighs the same as he did when he played pro ball, 210, only 10 pounds over his playing weight at Georgia. He works out three times a week, walking, riding his bicycle, and playing racquetball.

He owned and operated four Maryland Fried Chicken stores in Augusta for 20 years. Now he is down to one store and in two years hopes to be completely retired. Then he and Kay can spend more time with their four children, nine cats, three dogs, two horses, and two billy goats.

Meanwhile, Sapp is up at 7:00 AM five days a week. He works on his yard, checks his animals, and heads for his fried-chicken store, where he does everything from cooking to greeting the customers. When the lunch crowd is gone, he supervises the cleaning up, talks with his employees, checks the books, and heads for home. He and Kay rarely miss dinner together.

He has not attended a Bulldogs football game in four years, but he has never missed one on TV. "It is nice," he says, "to be able to avoid the traffic to and from Athens and to walk only a few steps from my den to the kitchen and have my own fried chicken."

What does he remember about breaking the drought? "On the bus trip from Athens to Grant Field, I remember telling Coach Butts that we were going to win the game. I told him I didn't sleep a wink last night, that all I could think about was that we were going to break the drought."

Sapp was born June 15, 1935, in Dublin, Georgia, the youngest of 10 children. When [Sapp] was three years old his father accidentally shot himself. His mother moved the family to Macon, where she supported the children by working as a riveter at Robins Air Force Base down the road in Warner Robins.

As he was at Georgia, Sapp was a 60-minute man on the Lanier High School football team. He played offensive fullback, backed up on the line on defense, kicked off, and returned punts and kickoffs. He led Lanier to the state Class AA championship and was picked to be on the All-State and All-Southern football teams.

He was recruited heavily by Auburn and South Carolina but had been listening to Georgia football on the radio since his preteen days. He signed a grant-in-aid with Georgia.

In the state's annual North-South High School All-Star football practice, his world came crashing down. In his first scrimmage, he drove into the defensive team's thickest part of the middle and was knocked head over heels in a major pileup, suffering three cracked vertebrae in his neck. His surgeon told him he should never play football again, that even a slight blow to the wrong place could be fatal.

Coaches Butts and Quinton Lumpkin came to the hospital and told Sapp he had his scholarship no matter what. He spent his entire freshman year at Georgia in a head-to-pelvis body cast. Coach Butts told him he should not play football again, but Sapp convinced his mentor otherwise. He spent his sophomore year on the B team and his junior and senior years on the varsity, bulling his way up the middle 258 times, right smack in the thick of things.

The Drought-Breaker flirted with death but became one of the greatest heroes in the history of University of Georgia football. Sound like fiction? It is the true story of a legend.

Bill Cromartie, *Clean, Old-Fashioned Hate*

1971: ANDY FOUND A WAY

Another unforgettable clash with Tech came on Thanksgiving Day 1971, the same day as the historic Oklahoma-Nebraska matchup. Also nationally televised, this game didn't have to take a backseat to the so-called Game of the Century when it came to thrills, as described in this chapter from Bill Cromartie's history of the Georgia–Georgia Tech rivalry.

Add one more to the list of names that Georgia and Georgia Tech football fans of age will *never* forget.

Add the name of Andrew Sidney Johnson, better known as Andy.

In the final 89 seconds of playing time at Grant Field, the Georgia sophomore quarterback put on one of the most exciting performances this colorful old rivalry has ever seen.

And the whole U.S.A. saw the memorable Thanksgiving night game via ABC-TV. The network hit a real jackpot that November 25. In the afternoon, its cameras were focused on the great Oklahoma-Nebraska national championship clash from Norman, Oklahoma, where the Huskers won it, 35–31.

The Georgia–Georgia Tech nightcap matched the earlier thriller, thrill for thrill, as the Bulldogs edged the Yellow Jackets at the wire, 28–24.

Not only was this the first nationally televised Tech-Georgia game, but also the first that was played on any day except a Saturday.

Even though Tech had defeated Georgia for the past two years, the Bulldogs entered the game as the hefty favorite. The Dogs were ranked number seven in the nation, losing only to Auburn 12 days earlier when quarterback Pat Sullivan, who won the 1971 Heisman Trophy, staged a fantastic air show that bombed the Red and Black, 35-20.

But Georgia's nine other foes were buried, 305–53.

Tech entered its Thanksgiving TV date with four straight wins and an overall record of 6–4–0, which included shutouts of Michigan State and Duke. However, the Jackets had to face the third-most prolific scoring team in Georgia's history, as offensive coordinator Fred Pancoast had his go-go boys averaging 33 points per game.

That scoring machine wasn't all Tech had to worry about, either. Coach Erk Russell's defensive platoon was seventh best in the country against scoring. Erk's Dogs had blanked Clemson, Vanderbilt, Kentucky, and South Carolina and limited Tulane, Mississippi State, Ole Miss, and Florida to only seven points each.

There was no doubt about it: Coach Bud Carson and his Yellow Jackets had a pack of "Wild Dogs" to deal with.

But Carson and his staff had the Jackets *ready*. They came out steaming and immediately took control of the game by scorching the stunned Bulldogs with two scores and a 14–0 lead.

The first time Tech got the ball, junior quarterback Eddie McAshan whipped his team to a touchdown. A five-play, 65-yard drive looked easy, and the payoff came on a 31-yard pass from McAshan to a wide-open Jim Owings in the end zone. Bobby Thigpen converted, and it was 7–0.

Late in the first period, Tech started another drive from its own 20, which ended when Rob Healey blasted over from the 11. Thigpen's PAT made it 14–0.

Tech, now fired sky-high, held Georgia and took over again, but the Bulldogs defense forced a punt that was downed at their 18. Jimmy Poulos and Johnson then led a long scoring march, capped by Andy's one-yard dive. After Kim Braswell's conversion, Georgia trailed 14–7 with 7:33 left in the first half.

However, it was enough time for 10 more points.

Tech's next possession resulted in a Bob Bowley punt that rolled dead on Georgia's 1-yard line. The Dogs punted it right back, and when Tech stalled at the 24, Cam Bonifay slammed a long field goal and a 17–7 advantage.

With the first-half clock down to 0:30, Georgia struck with a 23-yard TD pass from Johnson to Jimmy Shirer. Braswell converted, and the wild first half ended with the Yellow Jackets on the long side of a 17–14 score.

Many observers felt that Georgia had "won" the game with that score just before intermission.

"The score stunned Tech, and Georgia could now see the light of day," reported Harry Mehre of the *Atlanta Journal*.

After a scoreless third quarter, the TD fireworks began exploding again.

Early in the final period, Johnson sneaked over from the 1, Braswell kicked good, and the heavily favored Bulldogs were *finally* on top, 21–17, and now seemed more than able to kiss their pesky opponents off to beddie-bye.

The lead lasted no time at all.

Tech returned the kickoff to its 33 and, in five plays, was back on top. Healey ripped off a 12-yarder, then seven more, before Tim Macy got three and a first down at Georgia's 45. McAshan threw to Mike

Oven for 35 yards; Healey ran for 10. Touchdown. Thigpen toed true, and it was 24–21 with 10:30 left to play.

The score shocked the Bulldogs, and their fans, into the harsh reality that they were indeed dangerously close to the pains of losing to Tech for the third-straight year. And Grant Field was being eaten alive by roars of madness.

Tech kicked off...Georgia punted...Tech punted...and the Bulldogs were in good shape at their own 49 with just over seven minutes remaining. Johnson gained six yards before Robert Honeycutt broke off a 16-yarder to the Jackets' 29. Johnson got five, Shirer six and a first down at the 18.

Folks were going crazy, not only at the stadium, but also in front of TV sets.

Honeycutt hammered for another five, Poulos three, and Johnson one, bringing up fourth-and-one at the 9.

Tech stingerback Dave Beavens broke through and slammed Johnson for a loss of four yards. The Yellow Jackets had blunted the Bulldogs' big threat and reclaimed the football with only 3:38 to play.

Grant Field was now rocking all the way down to its ancient foundation.

Tech couldn't move and punted—but what a punt it was. Bowley, standing in his own end zone, boomed a beauty all the way to Georgia's 35-yard line.

As Georgia's 11 offensive players stood waiting through a commercial timeout, all that could be seen was their own facebars, a clock that showed only 1:29, 65 long yards of green carpet, and 11 fire-eyed Tech defenders.

Andy Johnson went to work.

After throwing incomplete, the "supersoph" broke free for 22 yards and a first down at Tech's 43.

Johnson, now being harassed by Tech's onrushing front four and faced with a defensive web which included seven more Yellow Jackets, threw incomplete.

Second-and-10, 1:08 left.

He threw incomplete again.

Third-and-10, 1:03 left.

He threw incomplete again.

Fourth-and-10, 0:57 left.

Frantic thoughts were also swirling through Bud Carson's mind at this precise moment. He was under heavy pressure from Tech alumni, and here he stood, only one down away from "saving" his job as head coach for at least another year. After all, how could Tech fire a coach who had upset Georgia three straight years? *One play!*

The Georgia team broke from the huddle. Johnson barked the signals across the line of scrimmage, took the snap from center

Kendall Keith, and the two big lines smashed head-on. He spotted tight end Mike Greene in the middle. Andy fired away, hitting Greene for an 18-yard gain and a first down at Tech's 25.

Time: 0:48.

Johnson then passed complete to split end Lynn Hunnicutt on the sideline and out of bounds at the 15, but just shy of a first down.

Time: 0:36.

Johnson came back with the exact same play to Tech's 9. First-and-goal.

Time: 0:31.

Stan Beavers, a wreckerback, trapped Johnson for a big loss of four yards, back to the 13, as Johnson quickly called Georgia's final timeout.

Time: 0:28.

Johnson went back to the sideline for final instructions from the coaching staff, came back out, and immediately hit Shirer just inside the 1. Shirer stepped out of bounds, stopping the clock.

Time: 0:18.

It was third down when Johnson handed off to Poulos, and the "Greek Streak" hurdled up and over a two-and-a-half-ton mass of humanity.

Touchdown!

Time: 0:14.

Poulos barely made it. Had he been short, Tech would have hung on for victory, even though Georgia had another play. There was no way in the world the Jackets would have let themselves get untangled. ...

Braswell's conversion wasn't even noticed.

Final score: Georgia 28, Tech 24.

Georgia Bulldogs nationwide went *crazy, crazy, crazy!*

The 66th game between the two state rivals had been one of the most exciting or devastating—depending upon which side your colors were flying that Thanksgiving night in 1971.

Mehre wrote, "Both teams played so brilliantly that a tie game probably would have been the right answer."

On a visit to the Tech dressing room, the *Journal's* Jim Huber reported, "It is quiet. Middle of the night quiet. Like 3:00 AM on a dark backstreet.

"Only the shower spray is audible.

"Burly linemen hold bleeding faces under hot water to wash away the blood and tears.

"Some said, 'Now I know how Oklahoma felt today.'"

"And on the other side," wrote Furman Bisher, "many a shriek shrieked. Backs slapped. Necks hugged. Whistles whistled. And the Lord thanked. Georgia hadn't been so happy to win one from Tech since Theron Sapp broke the drought in 1957."

Georgia led in first downs (24–15) and total yards (415–301). For the fourth year in a row, Tech came out with more penalty yards (40–20). Poulos was the game's leading rusher with 152 yards in 19 carries, while Healey had 130 yards in 24 attempts. Johnson was 9 for 19 in passing for 107 yards, and he ran for another 99, giving him a total of 206 for the night. McAshan had 118 air yards via 13 completions.

The series standings now showed figures of 32–29–5, Bulldogs.

Georgia went on to the Gator Bowl, where Vince Dooley's Dogs defeated brother Bill Dooley's North Carolina Tar Heels, 7–3. It was the first time brothers had ever opposed each other as head coaches in a bowl game.

The Bulldogs finished the season with an 11–1–0 record, their best in 25 years. Dooley's 1971 team became the third in Bulldogs history to win as many as 11 games.

It was reported that the Tech players had rejected a Peach Bowl bid. However, some "outside pressure" was put on the team for a revote. One was taken, the Peach was accepted, and in a few weeks, the Jackets went down the street to Atlanta Stadium and got wiped out in a driving rainstorm by Ole Miss. The score was 41–28, but it could have been much worse had Rebels coach Bruiser Kinard so desired.

That was Bud Carson's last game as head coach at Georgia Tech. He finished five years at the Flats with a 27–27–0 record.

Dan Magill, *Athens Banner-Herald*

GOFF PLAYED INCREDIBLE GAME AGAINST FLORIDA

The Georgia-Florida rivalry has featured its share of memorable games, as Dan Magill relates in this story prior to the 2003 renewal of the rivalry. His focus is on the 1976 game in which Ray Goff both runs and passes the Bulldogs to victory.

It's hard to single out the most memorable of the Georgia-Florida games I've seen these past 70 years. But perhaps the finest all-around performance (rushing and passing) ever rendered by a Bulldogs quarterback occurred November 6, 1976, in Jacksonville. A strapping south Georgian (6'2", 220 pounds) from Moultrie led Georgia to an unbelievable second-half comeback victory. His name: Ray Goff. It was a very important game in the race for the SEC championship. Florida was leading the SEC with a 4–0 record; Georgia was 3–1, having been upset at Ole Miss. The Gators rolled up an impressive 27–13 first-half lead, and it looked hopeless for the Bulldogs. But Georgia came back and played an absolutely flawless second half on offense and defense, shutting out the Gators 28–0 and limiting them to only three first downs. Final score: Georgia 41, Florida 27. Goff's stats that afternoon were fantastic: perfect in passing, going 5 for 5, including two touchdowns, and he rushed for a phenomenal 184 yards and three touchdowns. His 184 rushing total is still the Georgia single-game record for a quarterback. Goff was selected Quarterback of the Week by United Press. He went on to lead Georgia to the SEC title and was named SEC Player of the Year, becoming Georgia's first player to make the All-SEC first team at quarterback since Francis Tarkenton in 1960.

The most lopsided score in this long series, which began in Ocala in 1904 (Florida moved from Ocala to Gainesville in 1906), was Georgia's 75–0 win November 7, 1942, in Jacksonville. Heisman-winner Frank Sinkwich and his understudy at tailback, sophomore Charley Trippi, each accounted for four TDs. Sinkwich ran for two and passed for two (both to end George Poschner); Trippi had two long TD runs, passed for one (also to Poschner), and returned one interception for a touchdown. The next week against Chattanooga, Coach Wallace Butts put Trippi at number one tailback and moved Sinkwich to spinnerback (fullback). Although Auburn upset Georgia the next week, the Bulldogs rebounded in the finale, clobbering previously unbeaten Georgia Tech 34–0 to clinch their first SEC crown. On January 1, Georgia blanked UCLA, 9–0, in the Rose Bowl and claimed the national title. All-SEC safety Charlie Britt made two spectacular plays as Georgia beat Florida, 21–10, en route to the SEC crown. In the second quarter, the Gators' Richard Allen passed to their speedster Bobby Joe Green (who had been clocked at 9.5 in the 100) and Britt overhauled him at the Georgia 2, where All-American Pat Dye deflected an Allen pass on fourth-and-seven at the 11. Britt scooped it up at the goal line and raced 100 yards to glory, clinching the victory.

Herschel Walker was at his incredible best versus Florida en route to three straight conference championships. All Bulldogs fans remember the 1980 Buck Belue–Lindsay Scott 93-yard TD pass in the closing moments of a 26–21 comeback victory, but may have forgotten that Herschel Walker drew first blood on Georgia's first possession with a 72-yard touchdown jaunt. He finished with 238 yards rushing. In 1981 Georgia won by the same score, 26–21, with Walker tallying all four scores (the first two on passes of 24 and 16 yards from Belue, the last two on four- and one-yard runs). Walker led a sensational 95-yard drive for the winning score, gaining 65 himself, the last a one-yard plunge for the TD. His rushing total was 191 yards. In his swan song against the Gators, he shredded the Florida defense for 219 yards rushing (three touchdowns) in a 44–0 cakewalk. His totals in three games against Florida were 648 yards rushing and eight touchdowns, six on rushes, two on pass receptions.

Although Georgia holds a commanding lead in the series (45–34–2), the Bulldogs have won only once in the past 12 years. It took place in Coach Jim Donnan's second year and snapped a seven-game losing streak to Florida. Future NFL stars Hines Ward (Pittsburgh) and running back Robert Edwards (New England) paced the 37–17 upset over number-six Florida. Edwards rushed for 124 yards and scored on runs of 27, one, one, and 37 yards. Ward, who was the SEC offensive back of the week, accounted for 203 total yards (seven catches for 85 yards, five rushes for 21, two pass completions for 27, and two kickoff returns for 70). Furthermore, quarterback Mike Bobo threw for 260 yards (16 of 27), and he is still with the Bulldogs as Coach Mark Richt's quarterbacks coach. He and Richt (when [Richt] was offensive coordinator at FSU) have firsthand experience beating the Gators.

Blake Giles, *Athens Banner-Herald*

NATIONAL CHAMPIONS

Despite being outgained and completing only one pass all afternoon, Dooley's boys finished with a perfect 12–0 in the 1981 Sugar Bowl against Notre Dame.

Every week this year in Gameday, we have republished game stories from Georgia's 1980 national title season. This is a recap of the Bulldogs' season-ending victory over Notre Dame in the Sugar Bowl on January 1, 1981. On January 2, 1981, the Bulldogs were rewarded their only AP national title.

Say what you want to about the Georgia football team, but say this: the Bulldogs are 12–0 and number one in the nation.

The doubters and critics may say what they will, but after Georgia defeated Notre Dame 17–10 in the 1981 Sugar Bowl here in the Superdome, those same critics will find it difficult to deny the national championship to the only team in the country with a perfect record.

An improbable band of heroes climaxed an unexpected season and enriched a wealthy tradition with the first national title in any sport in the history of the school.

It may not have been a convincing win. In fact, the statistics were weighted heavily in favor of the losers, but it was a win nonetheless, accomplished in what has become typical fashion this year.

The punishing running of Herschel Walker was present as usual despite a shoulder injury suffered on the first possession, but it was the opportunistic play of Georgia's defense and kicking game that saved the day.

"This game was typical of the kind of games we have had against good opponents," said a beaming Coach Vince Dooley. "We just seem to find some way, somehow, to win.

"We may not be great in any phase of the game, but we are good in every phase. Some phase of the game finds a way to win."

On Thursday, the heroes of this win were all members of the Georgia secondary, though their level of contribution [in] the past runs the gamut from heavy to nonexistent.

Sure, Walker won the Miller-Digby Memorial Trophy, awarded to the game's most valuable player, but it was really Scott Woerner, Chris

Welton, Mike Fisher, Bob Kelly, Steve Kelly, and Terry Hoage who won this game.

They represent, respectively, an All-American cornerback, a senior rover decorated for academic and leadership accomplishments, a senior starting cornerback, a former starting defensive back banished to the specialty team, a former tailback co-regular switched to defense, and a freshman whose jersey had hardly been wrinkled in competition this year.

When the final whistle had been blown and when Dooley had made his way through the thousands of Bulldogs fans who swarmed the Superdome field, he received a call from President Jimmy Carter himself, a Georgia Tech alum talked into attending by his staff of Bulldogs alumni, none of whom could have gotten tickets, otherwise.

Well, everybody's a Bulldogs fan now, except maybe for the people in Pittsburgh and Norman, Oklahoma, who still doubt the validity of Georgia's claim. Notre Dame is convinced.

"Georgia is 12–0, and they're one of the top teams we played," said linebacker Bob Crable. "They had the endurance to last the whole season, and that's what it takes to be number one."

Outgoing Notre Dame coach Dan Devine said: "Georgia has a great team. Georgia is a great national champion. They are by far the best football team we played this year. A lot of teams have won the national championship which didn't have as good a team as Georgia."

Dooley said: "I've got one vote [in the UPI poll], and I'm voting for Georgia." Informed that Devine agreed, Dooley chirped, "That's two!"

Georgia beat Notre Dame despite being outperformed in first downs, total yards, time of possession, and number of plays. And the Bulldogs completed just one pass all afternoon.

"I didn't think we could win with just one completion," marveled quarterback Buck Belue after a frustrating day.

By contrast, Notre Dame came out with a passing circus. The first drive of the day, which netted the Irish a 50-yard field goal by junior Harry Oliver was accomplished mainly on the arm of freshman Blair Kiel.

Georgia's first possession of the day was almost disastrous. On the second play, Walker, a freshman from Wrightsville, Georgia, swept right and promptly subluxated his left shoulder. In layman's terms, he popped it out of joint.

"The doctor was very concerned when he was looking at him," Dooley said. "I was thinking *this is not good*. We had to find some way to win, but it didn't look good."

Walker's shoulder popped back in. The rest of the day he carried the ball in his right arm. He gained 150 yards, but it took him 36 laborious carries, the longest for 23 yards. He scored both of the Bulldogs' touchdowns.

Two plays after Walker went out, another problem showed up which was to plague Georgia all day—the passing game, or lack thereof. On a third-and-16, Belue was sacked by sophomore Joe Rudzinski. Later it was freshman Tim Marshall who set up camp in the Georgia backfield.

"I've never before seen a rush like that one," admitted Belue. "They put a lot of pressure on us. They've got a lot of talent on defense."

Dooley said the Irish were better in the flesh than on celluloid.

"When Buck goes back to pass, our offensive line doesn't usually go back so fast with him," Dooley said.

The Fighting Irish seemed headed for yet another field goal when Oliver lined up for a 48-yard attempt, but unlikely hero Hoage crashed through to block the kick, giving Georgia field position at the Irish 49.

Georgia drove as deep as the 19, but eventually settled for a 46-yard field goal by senior All-American kicker Rex Robinson.

The ensuing kickoff had to be one of the strangest plays in the history of college football. Robinson lofted a high kickoff inside the Irish 5, where it went unfielded by either Ty Barber or Jim Stone.

Before Stone could recover, junior Steve Kelly had knocked him away so that brother Bob, a senior, could recover it on the 1. Two plays later, Walker was diving over for the touchdown. Robinson's kick made it 10–3.

On Notre Dame's first possession of the second quarter, sophomore fullback John Sweeney got his first call of the day. Sophomore Nate "Ty Ty" Taylor separated him from the football, allowing senior Welton to fall on it at the Irish 22.

Walker rammed for 12, Belue ran for seven, and Walker circled end for three to put the ball in the end zone, and Georgia went up 17–3 with 13:49 to go in the half. Georgia spent the rest of the game hanging on.

The Irish came right back on the next possession, now under the direction of senior Mike Courey. But on fourth-and-three, Courey tried an alley-oop to senior Pete Holohan, into the corner of the end zone. But Woerner intercepted in the zone and ran it back to the Georgia 19.

On the second play of the second half, Walker topped the 100-yard mark, but the play was symbolic, too, because it was Georgia's last honest first down until the final three minutes of the game. Meanwhile, the defense clung and clung.

Woerner robbed Holohan again, this time from Kiel, stripping him in the corner on a third-down play. Oliver missed a 30-yard field-goal attempt.

The Irish were not denied the next time, driving 57 yards in 10 plays. Sophomore Phil Carter dove over from the 1.

Oliver was wide on a 38-yard field goal later. Fisher then intercepted a Kiel pass at the Irish 37, but Georgia realized nothing.

The final big play came on a surprising pass play on fourth-and-one at the Georgia 43. The Irish elected to pass, and Woerner intercepted.

Georgia finally kept the ball for more than six plays, killing the final 2:56 with the help of its one pass completion of the day.

Herschel Walker, shown here during his Heisman Trophy–season of 1982—during which he rushed for 1,752 yards and made 17 touchdowns as a junior—may have been the greatest Bulldog of them all.

Section II
THE PLAYERS

Dan Magill, *Dan Magill's Bull-Doggerel*

THE IMMORTAL BOB McWHORTER

*Bob McWhorter could truly do it all—run, block, and pass. Here Dan
Magill profiles the Bulldogs' very first All-American Hall of Famer.*

When I used to travel the state to Georgia Bulldog Club meetings, fre-
quently I would be asked the question, "You've been around Georgia
so long, did you know Bob McWhorter?" To which I would reply, "Did
I know Bob McWhorter! Why, I'll have you know that I played in the
same backfield with Bob McWhorter," which was no lie. I did play in
the same backfield with Bob McWhorter Jr. (Marse Bob's son), in intramural football at Georgia just prior to World War II.

I never had the pleasure of seeing Bob McWhorter play football (his
last game for Georgia in 1913 was eight years before I was born), but I
did know Mr. Bob and many members of the large and distinguished
McWhorter clan. The original McWhorters, by the way, came to
Delaware from Ireland, in the early days of this country, then migrated
on down to Virginia and North Carolina and eventually to Georgia.

Both Bob's father and grandfather (the original Robert Ligon
McWhorter for whom Bob was named) graduated from Georgia. Bob
was born in Lexington, Georgia, only 15 miles from Athens, on June 4,
1891, but his boyhood home was the McWhorter plantation "big
house" located on the highest ground of what is now Cloverhurst
Avenue in Athens, which was just three short blocks from my boyhood
home on Cherokee Avenue. And my present home on Woodlawn was
built on land where Judge Hamilton McWhorter (Bob's father) planted
cotton for many years, the same cotton fields where young Bob played
as a boy and was so fast (according to his younger brother Howard)
that he could run down rabbits.

All five of Judge McWhorter's sons were good athletes at Georgia:
Marcus, Hamilton Jr., and Howard excelled in baseball; Bob and
Thurmond (the youngest) in football. Bob also starred in baseball,
being considered the South's best player (heavy-hitting center fielder),

and it was believed he could have been an outstanding professional player like his contemporary and fellow north Georgian, Ty Cobb of nearby Royston. But Bob chose a career in law instead.

However, I did see Bob McWhorter play baseball. That is, I saw him play softball on old Herty Field in the late 1930s when Mr. Bob was in his late 40s. It was a game between the UGA faculty all-stars (Mr. Bob taught law) and the fraternity league intramural all-stars, and Bob McWhorter hit the longest softball home run I have ever seen. Home plate was in front of the chapel bell, and Mr. Bob smacked the ball over the center fielder's head, past the old Beanery (now the School of Landscape Architecture and Environmental Design), and all the way to Lumpkin Street.

Yes, I certainly did know Bob McWhorter, but not as well as my father (editor of the *Athens Banner-Herald*), who was one of [McWhorter's] closest friends and was instrumental in getting Mr. Bob to run for mayor, an office he held for many years, did. And it was by far the biggest honor of my life to represent my deceased father as a pallbearer at Mr. Bob's funeral at the First Baptist Church in June 1960.

Bob McWhorter was unarguably Georgia's greatest football player during our first half century of football. He was named All-Southern from 1910 through 1913, and during an era when it was almost impossible for a southerner to make the Yankee sportswriters' All-America teams, he became Georgia's first All-American in 1913.

The man who knew Bob McWhorter's football accomplishments best, his "Boswell," was the late Charlie Martin, who was in school at Georgia throughout McWhorter's brilliant career. And Charlie, who was an Athens sportswriter and newspaperman before becoming Georgia's business manager of athletics in the 1920s and early 1930s, many times regaled me with his hero's exploits. Some of the highlights I well remember:

- Bob McWhorter's first official athletic competition was at Gordon Military College in Barnesville, Georgia, where he played under Coach Alex Cunningham. Their baseball team came up to Athens one spring and beat Georgia, 11–0. Dr. S. V. Sanford, Georgia's faculty chairman of athletics, that same day hired Cunningham to be Georgia's football and baseball coach. Cunningham was a disciple of Dan McGugin, who had made Vanderbilt the football power in the South, and McGugin was a disciple of Fielding Yost, who had made Michigan the mightiest team in the land. Cunningham brought McWhorter to Georgia with him in the fall of 1910 as a freshman although Bob was just a junior at Gordon. Dr. Sanford wanted Bob at Georgia, so it was "arranged."

- Bob McWhorter led Georgia to victory over Georgia Tech his freshman year on the strength of a 45-yard run late in the game, which ended a five-year winning streak by the John Heisman–coached Yellow Jackets. This feat made McWhorter an instant Bulldogs hero, and he went on to lead Georgia to three more wins over Georgia Tech, an even more remarkable feat when it is realized that all games were played on the enemy's home field in Atlanta. Once McWhorter graduated, Tech and Heisman resumed their winning ways over Georgia.

- In 1913 in Atlanta, Tech dedicated its new stadium, Grant Field, by playing Georgia with a record crowd of 10,000 on hand. Heisman had devised a defense that he thought could stop McWhorter. His linemen slanted on their charges into the Bulldogs backfield toward McWhorter, and they did bottle him up most of the game. But Coach Cunningham countered by feeding the ball to another Bulldogs back, Stephen Crump, who had a field day. Georgia won, 14–0, with none other than Bob McWhorter scoring the final TD on a one-yard plunge. Tech students, by the way, were so confident that they would upset Georgia that they pledged not to shave until Christmas if they lost (the game was played November 15, almost six weeks before Christmas!).

- McWhorter graduated from Georgia with an A.B. degree in 1914, [was a member of] Phi Beta Kappa and Phi Kappa Phi, and was elected to Sphinx as a junior. He received his law degree from Virginia in 1917, and while he was at Virginia, the Cavaliers went up to Boston to play perennial national champion Harvard. There the Boston sportswriters wrote that Virginia had a mysterious halfback by the name of "Bob White," who was the best runner they had ever seen. It is said that "Bob White" was really Bob McWhorter, but Mr. Bob never admitted it to me. He always merely smiled when I asked him about this story. But it is well known that in the old days schools often played "ringers."

- McWhorter's main asset as a football player was his ball-carrying ability, but he was a good all-around player, excelling on defense and also as a blocker and passer. He was powerfully built (about 5'10", 185 pounds with a lot of strength in his legs and hips—like Frank Sinkwich), and he had very good speed. Georgia didn't pass much, but McWhorter won several games with his passing. In his day a player could pass out of bounds in lieu of punting, and Bob had the strongest arm of any player in Dixie. His most famous pass beat Auburn on Thanksgiving Day in Athens in 1912. It was fourth down, the score tied 6–6 late in the game, when McWhorter went back to pass out of bounds instead of punting, but the ball slipped in his hand and didn't go out of bounds. Instead, a surprised end, Hugh Conklin, caught it in the end zone for the winning score. Bob liked to tell this story about his greatest pass.

Bob McWhorter scored 61 touchdowns during his four seasons at Georgia. The school record is listed as 52 by one Herschel Walker, and it should be corrected. Bob McWhorter was Georgia's first inductee into the National Football Foundation's Hall of Fame, and it is most appropriate that the Bulldogs' athletic dormitory is named for this modest and most gifted athlete, Athens's most revered son.

Dick Jemison, *Atlanta Constitution*

BOB M'WHORTER

For an account of Bob McWhorter's heroics back in his playing days,
here is an article from the October 5, 1913, edition of the Atlanta
Constitution *as McWhorter headed into his senior season.*

"'Nuf Sed."

This sizes up the football situation at the University of Georgia for
the season of 1913, as briefly as one could possibly express it.

Psychologically, this sizing up really does what it purports to do.

Bob McWhorter is the last word in football in Athens. When you
mention football to an Athens fan, its definition is Bob McWhorter,
and vice versa.

Bob Will Be Star

Bob is going to have the greatest season of his wonderful career on the
gridiron, or I am no judge of the early form of a football player.

Bob was a sick man at the start of last season, and this illness
detracted considerably from his work for the season. But sick, Bob was
good enough to earn an All-Southern halfback berth, so you can see
what I mean when I say he's "right."

The entire attack of the Georgia team will be centered around their
star, and if they did not center it around him they would be overlooking their best bet.

Do not misunderstand me. Bob is not going to be given all the
work to do. He is willing enough and all that, and he will be entrusted
with the duty of gaining the necessary yardage when it is absolutely
imperative.

What I mean is this: McWhorter is the star of the Red and Black
team, and as the star, every play that is made on the offense is going to
be shaped around him so as to get the most good therefrom—the best
results. He will be the hitching post that Georgia will tie her horse to.

Starting Faster

Bob is starting faster this year than ever before, yet at the same time he
is running in the same careful manner that he always ran, picking his
holes and then darting through them like a flash.

Captain Bob is going to be harder to head off under full steam this year than he ever was, and here we are right back where we started again.

When he does start with the ball he is going to be given the best interference that a halfback has ever received in the South.

Here comes your psychology stuff.

The Georgia team has confidence in Bob McWhorter. They know that when he is entrusted to carry the pigskin that nine times out of 10, nay, 99 out of 100, he is going to make a gain, in the majority a substantial one.

See the point? The efforts of the team will be concentrated in playing their one best bet to the finish and in furnishing him with the assistance permitted under the rules that will enable them to attain the object of their attack, a substantial gain—a possible touchdown, on a long-sweeping end run.

The old psychology stuff works out in the inspiration that McWhorter is to his teammates. He is a player that inspires confidence, a wish, as it were, to excel in the same manner that he does, a careful, painstaking study of the game itself.

Bob's Rating High

In short, Bob McWhorter's presence on the University of Georgia football team of 1913, and with the added impetus to be gained from the "Captain Bob" idea, will be of such inestimable value that one cannot set it down in figures.

A few years ago at Tech they referred to John Davis as "Old Twenty Percent." He was considered that much of the team.

Without reflecting on the ability of any other member of the Georgia team Bob's rating is, in my humble estimation, several degrees higher.

But we'll see Bob in action in Atlanta at least three times this season, and you can judge for yourself. Bob McWhorter is an interesting football study, and his value to the red and black team cannot be fully expressed in mere words, or even figures, so we'll take a little analytic study of what other potent factors the red and black 1913 team shows.

The team as a whole is there [skilled and prepared]. A little later in the season, when they get polished up on their signals, a little more team play, and the regular lineup working daily, that word "there can be spelled with a capital *T*."

Not Far Advanced

At this stage of the season, compared with the same stage of the season last year, the present team does not look as good, but to be honest, this will be rather a help than a hindrance.

The answer is simple. Last year's team was boosted so high that when they did fall, it was heartbreaking. This year's team has not been boosted as highly. Result: it is creating a spirit among the men that will bring surprising results.

Georgia's 1912 season was a success. Any Georgia season is a success when Tech and Auburn are both defeated. If this year's team accomplishes the same, what they do in the other games will be forgotten entirely.

But Georgia is not going to be forgotten in the other games. She is going to leave something with the other teams that they will remember, and we include in this the Virginia crowd that everyone is fearing so. The winner of this game we would not forecast anymore than we would attempt to predict the outcome of the Georgia-Tech game.

Either would be suicidal from a scribe standpoint—but Virginia is going to know she had a football game when she leaves that field in Atlanta on October 25, regardless of result.

But I am deviating from the main point at issue. Let's take a look at the individual players.

In the Backfield
Captain Bob McWhorter will play one halfback. He'll play it. Further comment is unnecessary.

Dave Paddock, looking better than ever, is back and will be the field general of the team. And Dave is our choice for All-Southern quarterback without seeing any of the others in action. This boy has the goods, and he will deliver them in large bundles.

Paddock is the ideal build for a quarterback. He weighs, I should say, about 150 to 155 pounds, is fast as a deer, knows a lot of football, and knows how to size up the proper play at the proper time.

Around Paddock will center a lot of Georgia's attack. He'll direct the play, and the good headwork that he showed last season is a sample of what he can be expected to do this year. He'll get the most good out of the resources at his command. You can gamble on that point.

I understand that Paddock is no slouch as a drop kicker and punter, though maybe I am divulging a state secret by letting the world know this, but nevertheless here it is and with these many good points he will make a formidable field general.

Powell at Full
[John] Powell will be the regular fullback. He was last season, and he is going to be again this year, with a year's experience, more ability gained by such experience, and a little better developed speed.

For his weight, this fellow looks to weigh about 160 pounds; he hits the line mighty hard, and he has the knack of hitting it low, a faculty of keeping his feet when hit and stumbling along for a few extra yards before being sat on.

At the other halfback, in our humble opinion, this young fellow Carey is going to be Bob McWhorter's running mate. Carey has not played any football since he was on the Gordon [Military College] team with Bob McWhorter a few years ago. But this will be a good point in his favor. He knows Bob's style of play and ought to fit in well.

Carey is built a little like Jene Patten at Tech, though not as square of shoulder and probably about five pounds lighter, but he is a better man than old reliable Timeon Bowden, and Georgia boys know how reliable [he] was.

He's fast as the proverbial blue streak and circles the ends with dazzling speed. Incidentally, he can hit that line pretty well, though he start in off tackle smashes better than in anything he does.

Thompson v. Carey

Charlie Thompson, the former Boys' High schoolboy, is running Carey a great race for the position, and many prefer Thompson to Carey, but the latter had them sitting up and taking notice during scrimmage the past week.

The battle is going to be between these two, though there are some other first-string men, their main weakness being their lack of weight. But these fellows will be carried on the squad and used.

They are Corley, the baseball pitcher; [Edwin] Broyles, an Atlanta boy and a nephew of Judge Briles; and Holtzclaw, a former Boys' High School lad.

[H. William Sidberry], who played fullback for Riverside Military Academy last season, will be a sub for Powell at the fullback position.

There are several other quarterbacks out, all of whom are very light. [Walker] Flournoy and [W. H.] McLaws can probably be eliminated without further discussion, though they show promise for another season, with increasing weight.

The two lightweights that are attracting attention and who will be retained on the squad are Ed Dorsey of last year's team and Holland, who played quarterback for Gordon last season.

Holland will run the scrubs all season. He may get into some games, but it is doubtful, unless a condition arises that is not looked for by any of Georgia's enemies, the crippling of all the heavy material present.

One Hundred Eight Pounds of Nerve

"Little Ed" Dorsey will be assistant to Paddock, and this little rascal will take part in a part of every game that Georgia plays during the season. Despite his light weight—he tips the beam at but 108 pounds—he is easily the pick of the backfield men, regardless of weight, except the four regulars we mentioned above.

Dorsey is an inspiration to any team. He fights harder with that 108 pounds than most of the players with the last two figures reversed. He is a fierce tackler. He demonstrated that to Atlanta fans by the way he pulled down Lewie Hardage in the Vanderbilt game last season.

Dorsey is 108 pounds of pepper and nerve, and the team [absorbs] it from him. Paddock's superior physique and knowledge of the game is all that keeps his position secure from Georgia's "Kid Woodruff Number Two."

At center are two corking good men, with beef galore, good speed for big men, and accurate passing ability, the last being the most essential in a good center.

Delaperriere to Guard

Arthur Delaperriere, the regular center on the 1911 team, is back and is the logical man for the place by reason of his previous experience, but he is not going to play there.

[D. T.] McKinnon, who weighs about 180 pounds, a scrub last season, kept off the varsity by the one-year rule, will be Georgia's regular snapper. And he answers all requirements. No further comment is necessary.

But what of Delaperriere, you say? Easy. He is going to be one of the regular guards of the team during the coming campaign, although he is doing the snapping during the scrimmage thus far.

At the other guard there is going to be a merry battle waged, with [James] Conyers, who played in several games last season; [Jones] Purcell, a scrub last season; Brown and Rutherford, also scrubs last season; and [Tom] Thrash, of Gordon, as the candidates.

This is where Georgia is richest in material, and Cunningham is not letting the grass grow under his feet. He is practicing all those follows as both guards and tackles and will have good available subs for the center of the line in case of injury at any stage of the game.

Of the five men mentioned for this other guard position, Conyers, at the present writing, probably has the inside track on the position and will probably be seen at that position all season, unless some unforeseen accident occurs or some of the new men improve more than they have shown. But all of these men will be kept on the squad and will get into a part of some of the games.

The Tackles

"Tiny" Henderson is a tackle certainty, and everyone knows how good Tiny's 210 pounds of bone and muscle is. It's All-Southern caliber this year, with Tom Brown at the other, and he and Brown would have an awful battle. To the football students such a description of Henderson is sufficient.

[Kirby] "Punk" Malone may hold down the other position. We use the word *may* advisedly, for Punk has not got his job cinched by any means. He's got a fight on his hands, and a warm one, too.

If [Bright] McConnell, a scrub a couple of years ago, is ruled eligible by the SIAA (Southern Intercollegiate Athletic Association), he and Henderson will probably be the choices for tackle. McConnell has everything that Henderson has, and the two will give Georgia a pair of tackles that will give them all plenty of trouble.

Then there is [Paul] Turner, who was at Tech two years ago, and a mighty good man. Such a good man that he is making the [battle] very keen for the other contestants. And he is willing. That is making [him] a hit with his coach.

The tackle crop is rather light, as you see, but what it lacks in quantity it make up in quality.

There are a slew of ends out, with Conklin, the veteran of last year's team and one of the best defensive ends that ever stepped on a southern gridiron as the only certainty of the lot.

Many Ends

[William Edgar] Hitchcock, who played last season; Smith, the former Riverside star; Howard McWhorter, captain of the Gordon [Military College] team last season and a brother of Captain Bob's; [Albert] Peacock, of basketball fame; Crump, a sub end last season; and Owens, the Eleventh Cavalry boy, are the end candidates.

To pick the man who will land this berth is a task and one that we will consign to Coach Cunningham, as they all look pretty good.

But what little I saw of these fellows in action. Young Smith, from Riverside, struck me as the best man of the lot. He's light. It is true, but he makes up for this by his uncanny intuition in sizing up where a play is going and getting into it.

Playing on the scrubs against the varsity last week he showed such promise that Coach Cunningham shifted him over to the varsity, where he has been starring ever since.

With a good, live tackler backing him up, Smith can be counted upon to dump the interference that starts around his end and leave it up to this other man to get the man with the ball, though he showed that even with his light weight he was equal to the combined task on several occasions.

I do not think that I will miss my guess very far when I say that Conklin and Smith will be the regular ends for Georgia this season with the possibility of Crump beating the latter out for the place by reason of more experience and weight.

Owens, the soldier boy, is showing great promise and is fast as a streak. He has plenty of grit and determination, and the end positions of the Georgia team are going to be benefited by this fellow's presence on the squad, as he is giving all the candidates a merry battle for the job.

Prospective Lineup

It will not take very much to size up a prospective line for the Red and Black, though, of course, it is subject to change with local conditions, college rules, injuries, etc., and no one is infallible especially in forecasting what a football coach will decide on as a permanent lineup, and their ideas of a good man are likely to be entirely different from the writer's.

This was shown in the case of Vanderbilt last season. Many thought that McGugin pulled a bone when he played Wilson Collins in the backfield and let Shay stand on the sideline.

Here's my dope on a permanent lineup for the Red and Black: McKinnon, center; Delaperriere and Conyers, guards; Henderson and Malone, tackles (McConnell as choice for Malone's place, if ruled eligible); Conklin and Smith or Crump, ends; Paddock, quarter; McWhorter and Carey, halfs; and Powell, full.

And this lineup would give them all a battle.

This lineup will be heavy enough, fast enough, and with enough experience.

Shown Weight, Too

This lineup will show an average of 175 pounds to the man. The line will average 180 pounds to the man and the back, field 166 pounds.

These weights are, of course, approximated, as at this time of year with the players having a little surplus flesh and accurate weights not being taken by the coach they are guess weights at best, but the weights given will not vary much, if any.

From tackle to tackle, the line will, when finally settled on, weigh 190 pounds average.

Total weights are, line from tackle to tackle, 950 pounds. Line from end to end, 1,262 pounds; backfield, 665 pounds; entire 11, 1,927 pounds.

Paddock, Carey, McWhorter, and Powell are all fast men in the backfield. Conklin and Smith, on the ends, are moderately fast, and for big men, the line from tackle to tackle has average speed.

In experience, the team does not lack much. Most of the players that are being counted on as regulars are either regulars or subs of last year's varsity or from last year's scrubs, and they all know Cunningham's system.

Kicking and Passing

For the punting end of the game, which is always a valuable asset to all good football teams, Georgia has four men who can be used in this capacity. Which one will eventually be decided upon, only improvement with practice alone can tell.

Powell, Thompson, Paddock, and Henderson are all able booting artists, with the last named probably able to get the most distance of the lot.

But as Henderson will play tackle and if Thompson is beaten out for a backfield position, he may be switched to end, in order to keep the kicking in the backfield without tipping the team's signal by bringing a man out of the line to punt, the kicking honors may settle on Powell and Paddock.

The former did most of the kicking in the latter part of the season last year, but Paddock is showing an aptitude to the punting game, and the little field general may be given the difficult task.

The forward passing is in able hands with Bob McWhorter hurling the pigskin, but Powell and Thompson are also being practiced at this art to insure against any possible injuries to the team's star.

With Powell, Thompson, Henderson, and Paddock to kick and McWhorter, Powell, and Thompson to forward pass, the Red and Black ought to have those departments of play well taken care of. In fact, no one seems to be worrying about their ability in this capacity.

Work Slowly

In closing, one point in particular: Cunningham has adopted a different system this year. His team is not going to hit its fastest clip early in the season and try to maintain it to the end like they did last year. These tactics were not a success.

Cunningham is going to work the team at easy stages and make the development slow.

Therefore, if one can say that the Georgia team is "there" in its present stages of development, what can be said when they are at the top of the game?

Last Sunday I wrote of the Tech team. Having seen both Tech and Georgia in action now, I can truthfully say that as far as predicting a winner is concerned, I am willing to toss a coin and take my pick. That's how closely they appear to be matched, judging of course, from their present form.

Marc Lancaster, *onlineathens.com*

NO. 3: UNIVERSITY OF GEORGIA ATHLETE OF THE CENTURY: FRANK SINKWICH

Georgia's first Heisman Trophy winner was Frank Sinkwich, who was selected in 1942. The story of his journey from Ohio to college stardom is presented in this article, which was part of a series picking the top Georgia athletes of the century.

Frank Sinkwich was the first player from the South to win the Heisman Trophy. He set SEC single-season records for rushing, passing, and total offense. He put together one of the best all-around performances ever in a bowl game. He was one of the greatest offensive players in college football history.

And he never would have come to the University of Georgia if Bill Hartman's car hadn't been low on gas.

It was the summer of 1939, and Hartman, backfield coach for Wally Butts, was on a recruiting trip in Ohio, a day-and-a-half drive from Athens, and things were not going well.

"We went there to contact the best back in Ohio, who was in Youngstown," Hartman said. "When we got there, the boy had already made up his mind to go to Ohio State. His name was Paul. ... I forget his last name now, but he went to Ohio State."

The long trip had apparently been made in vain until fate intervened.

"Coming back out of town, we stopped at a filling station to get some gas and got to talking to a filling-station attendant," Hartman said. "And he said, 'Well, the best back in the state really lives right down the street here, about three or four blocks.' We said, 'Who is that?' And he said, 'Well, that's Frank Sinkwich.'"

Hartman promptly turned the Plymouth around and headed for the Sinkwich residence, where he found the player's father sitting on the front porch. A few hours of conversation later, Frank Sinkwich of Chaney High School had agreed to make a recruiting visit to Athens later that summer—not that Hartman was aware of what he had stumbled upon.

By all accounts, Sinkwich was physically unremarkable. Certainly, there was no such thing as a 6'2", 210-pound running back in those days, but even among the smaller players of the day, the 5'10", 185-pound Sinkwich didn't stand out—until he touched the ball.

"Back at that time, you could do anything you wanted to with high school prospects," Hartman said. "We went out and got a ball and a center and we put [Sinkwich] at wingback first. We had some boys in summer school, and the center would snap the ball to the tailback and Sinkwich would come around and take it on a wingback reverse. Well, the thing that impressed us almost immediately was how quick he could start. We saw with that quickness that he could be a real good tailback in the single-wing, rather than as a wingback."

A Special Player

After that brief workout, Georgia's coaches knew they had uncovered a special player, and they were prepared to do anything they could to convince him to come to Georgia. But the only thing Sinkwich asked was that Georgia also offer a scholarship to his friend from Ohio, George Poschner, who had come on the trip with Sinkwich. The coaching staff didn't hesitate, and the Bulldogs had two more freshmen in line for that fall.

In those days, freshmen weren't eligible to play on the varsity; instead, they competed against other schools' freshmen a few times each fall. Sinkwich was an instant star for Georgia's Bullpups in the fall of 1939, leading the way as UGA scored like an arena football team on the way to an undefeated season. The group became known as the Point-a-Minute Bullpups, and Georgia's varsity coaches couldn't wait to get their hands on the freshmen the following year.

Even in practice, Sinkwich and his classmates were at times dominant—even Poschner, the throw-in player in the deal, made people look twice.

"As time went on, it became evident that Sinkwich was going to be a real good tailback and, surprisingly enough, Poschner was going to be a real good end," Hartman said. "In 1939, that was my first year coaching the backfield. Since I'd played with the Redskins the year before, I would go out there with what we called the 'Red Devil' [freshman] team and scrimmage the varsity. I could take the ball and pass because I had led the National Football League for a while in passing the previous year, so I would take old Poschner at the end and be in the middle, and he'd catch the ball and we'd score two or three touchdowns against the varsity.

"By the time they were playing Georgia Tech in the final freshman game of the year—which was always a big game, it was always played at Grant Field, and I guess we had 40,000 people there to see it—Sinkwich ran wild. He ran for a touchdown at one time, as I recall, I think there were 15 Tech men that tackled at him because some of them got up off the ground and had a second shot at him. He made a tremendous run—that was before you had many Polish or Croatian names, and Frank was Croatian—and the public address announcer was saying 'That guy Spankovich is at it again.' He gained a whole lot of publicity there."

When the fall of 1940 rolled around, everyone knew about Sinkwich. On the first day of practice, September 2, a crowd of several hundred gathered to watch the varsity work out "under a boiling sun."

As the next day's *Athens Banner-Herald* reported: "Though considerably overweight—a factor that has caused considerable concern among alumni—Frankie Sinkwich showed the crowd and the coaches he still has his old hip-shaking ability as he raced through holes."

Sinkwich soon got himself into shape, and an article in the September 12, 1940, edition of the *Banner-Herald* noted that Butts had six sophomores penciled into the starting lineup, including Sinkwich at tailback. That article, by young sportswriter Dan Magill, reported that Sinkwich had bumped juniors Heyward Allen and Hank Powers down to second- and third-string, respectively.

There were still some adjustments to make, though. Sinkwich had good running instincts, with the aforementioned quick start being his strongest asset. But playing tailback in the single-wing set required a bit more skill—Sinkwich had to learn how to pass.

"His sophomore year, by that time, we had taught him to throw the optional run-pass out of the single-wing," Hartman said. "He could run out there and jump up and throw that running pass. It was strictly optional, depending on what the defense did. If they stayed back, he ran; if they came up, he threw."

His throws weren't a thing of beauty by anyone's standards, but as time went on, the mere threat of Sinkwich pulling the ball down and running made him a more dangerous passer.

"He was mainly an effective passer because he could fake the run," Magill said. "They were so scared of him running that he could detect them if they came in too close, and he could find somebody open to complete a pass. He was effective for that reason; he wasn't the great type of passer that you see now as quarterbacks."

But he was good enough.

Sinkwich's varsity career didn't start with a bang. By the time the season opener against Oglethorpe University rolled around, Sinkwich had lost his starting position. Butts decided to go for more experience at the important position, and Sinkwich carried only one time for 15 yards as a substitute against Oglethorpe. But the next week against South Carolina, he ran for two long scores and threw for another.

After strong performances against Columbia and Kentucky in the next two games, Sinkwich earned the starting nod against Auburn on November 2, and he threw one touchdown pass. The boy from Youngstown was clearly on the right track, but his performance in the penultimate game of the year against Georgia Tech put to rest any doubts that he could become one of the best players in UGA's nearly 50 years of football.

On the Thursday of the week of the Tech game, Sinkwich was laid up in his dorm room with a 104-degree temperature. Two days later, he single-handedly drove Georgia to a 21–19 win over its biggest rival, carrying the ball 28 times for 128 yards and throwing a pair of touchdown passes. It was the Bulldogs' first win over the Yellow Jackets since 1936, and Sinkwich earned everyone's respect for his part in it.

According to Magill's story in the next day's *Banner-Herald*, "Sinkwich's amazing running caused George Webb, Tech's star right end, to come into the Bulldogs' dressing room after the game and say, 'Sinkwich, you're the greatest ballplayer I've ever seen.'

"Claude Bond, Tech's trainer, stopped newsmen as they were leaving the gymnasium and said: 'Our boys just told me that this Sinkwich is the best and the cleanest football player they've ever played against. I wish you'd put that in the paper because I think it is the truth. Our boys said that guy's interested in only one thing—getting that extra yard.'"

That victory, and another in the season finale against Miami a week later, helped Georgia finish the season with a winning record at 5–4–1.

High Expectations

Big things were expected of the Bulldogs as the 1941 season approached. Those who had made up the core of the 1939 freshman team were now upperclassmen, and a strong senior class led by Allen, who would go on to form one of Athens's most successful car dealerships, was in place. Much like the modern schedule, the Bulldogs started out with Mercer, a nonconference patsy. The Bulldogs demolished the Bears 81–0 as Sinkwich ran for three scores and passed for another.

Next up was South Carolina, which was not an SEC school at the time, in a game that would be another turning point in Sinkwich's career. As told in Magill's book *Dan Magill's Bull-Doggerel*, Georgia led 27–6 in Sanford Stadium late in the game when Sinkwich had his second run-in with South Carolina defender Steve Novak.

"I had received a hard lick to my jaw—in the same place—in the first quarter on the handoff to our fullback," Sinkwich recalled. "I carried out a fake, and the South Carolina end, Novak, gave me a forearm to the jaw.

"On my last play of the game, though, I faked a pass and ran a good way, almost scoring. Cramps hit my legs, and I buckled. I was run out of bounds and someone piled on, hitting my jaw again with a knee. I think it was the same Novak. South Carolina was penalized to the 1-yard line for unnecessary roughness, and we scored immediately.

"When I returned to the sidelines, Coach Butts asked me what ailed me, and I replied that I had a loose tooth. He commented: 'Oh. That's nothing!'"

Actually, Sinkwich had broken his jaw. With a huge game against Ole Miss the next week, this was not good news. Team dentist Dr. Jimmy Allen (Heyward's older brother) wired Sinkwich's jaw shut, and Sinkwich flew to Knoxville, Tennessee, to be checked out by Tennessee trainer Mickey O'Brien, in hopes that some protective headgear could be designed so he could play.

Allen and Georgia's medical staff began work on a helmet, but it wouldn't be ready in time for the Ole Miss game. So Sinkwich got a local machinist to make him a metal chin strap for protection against the Rebels, and he started the game with his jaw wired shut. Sinkwich ended up rushing for 98 yards and throwing a touchdown pass despite the difficulties caused by his injury. The teams tied, 14–14.

"The worst thing was trying to breathe through wired teeth," he said of the game. "I recall our trainer coming on the field with pliers to tighten up the wires which would get loose. There was no free substitution then, and I had to remain in the game if I wanted to continue playing."

Sinkwich's special helmet was ready for the next game against Columbia, and he played the rest of the year with a large jaw protector attached to his helmet.

He seemed to get stronger as the season progressed. In a 27–14 loss against Alabama the week after the Columbia game, Sinkwich ran for 109 yards. It was the first of five straight games in which he rushed for more than 100 yards, culminating in a 155-yard effort against Dartmouth on November 22.

A week later, Georgia Tech held him to 64 yards rushing, but he made up for it by throwing for 197 yards and three touchdowns in a 21–0 win at Grant Field.

Sinkwich's regular-season yardage totals were unprecedented. His 1,103 yards rushing set an SEC record, which stood for eight years, and his 1,816 yards of total offense set another conference standard. He earned All-America honors and finished fourth in the Heisman Trophy voting.

Better still, the Bulldogs wrapped up the year with an 8–1–1 record and earned a trip to the Orange Bowl against Texas Christian in their first-ever postseason appearance. It was before a record crowd of 35,786 fans in Miami that Sinkwich gained serious publicity outside the Southeast for the first time.

Sinkwich had the ball in his hands on every play of the game, slicing apart the Horned Frog defense at will. After Georgia took a 7–0 lead on a 2-yard run by Ken Keuper, Sinkwich took over. Before the quarter was out, he fired a 61-yard touchdown pass to Melvin Conger and a 60-yarder to Cliff Kimsey. In the second quarter, Sinkwich hit Lamar Davis for a 15-yard score, helping Georgia take a 33–7 halftime lead. Sinkwich added a 43-yard touchdown run for Georgia's final tally in the third quarter. He finished the day completing nine of 13 passes for 243 yards. He also rushed 139 yards and accumulated 382 yards of total offense and four touchdowns.

Sinkwich's touchdown run came on his signature play, in which he took the snap, faked a handoff, and went up the middle. The play, which exploited Sinkwich's starting speed, produced 25 of the 30 rushing touchdowns Sinkwich scored in his Georgia career.

"Spin 87 was his favorite play," Hartman said. "We'd trap the defensive guard with the blocking back, and [Sinkwich] did a half-spinner to the wingback and fullback coming around. Then he came up to cut in behind that trap and they were cross-blocking at the line of scrimmage, and we pulled the strong-side end through the hole ahead of him. He was virtually unstoppable on that play because he got there so quick.

"We were scrimmaging out there one day against the first-team defense, and we had Bill Godwin backing up the right side of the line, who weighed about 235 and was a pretty good linebacker. Sinkwich was in the huddle with Coach Butts, and Coach Butts said to Godwin, 'We're going to run spin 87 right at you; can you stop it?' And Godwin said yeah, he could. And [Butts] told Sinkwich that—he said, 'Yeah, he can stop you.' So we ran spin 87 right at Godwin, and Sinkwich hit him and walked right up his chest, knocked him down, and did a tattoo on him with those quick feet and ran about 40 yards."

It was a feeling most defenders got used to over the course of Sinkwich's career.

Bigger Expectations

Georgia's success in 1941 raised expectations to an almost unheard-of level for the next season. The Point-a-Minute Bullpups were now seniors, and everyone knew about Sinkwich. Avid Georgia fans were excited that he would be joined in the backfield by the previous year's star freshman player, a youngster named Charley Trippi.

As many of their contemporaries were sent overseas to fight in World War II, the Bulldogs prepared for what many expected to be their finest season ever. Things went as planned from the start, even though they opened the season with a nail-biting 7–6 win at Kentucky.

Georgia won its first nine games as Sinkwich led the way with an even more balanced effort than he had given the year before. A 35–13 win at Cincinnati on October 24 was Sinkwich's statistical high point. He rushed for 136 yards and three touchdowns and threw for 227 yards, including touchdown passes of 90 (which is still the fifth-longest in UGA history) and 80 yards to Lamar Davis.

The five-score performance is still the best single-game effort in school history. Ray Goff tied the mark against Florida in 1976, as did Robert Edwards against South Carolina in 1995. Sinkwich finished 1942 with 27 touchdowns, a mark that still stands—the closest anyone else has come is Eric Zeier's 25-touchdown performances in 1993 and 1994.

Georgia rolled until it suffered its first loss of the year against Auburn on November 21. The Tigers held Sinkwich to just 31 yards rushing, his second-lowest output in the final two years of his career. The only lower point came in 1942 against the Jacksonville Naval Air Station, when Sinkwich was knocked out on the game's fourth play with a bruised pelvis.

Sinkwich and Georgia didn't let the disappointment of the Auburn loss bother them. The Bulldogs bounced back the next Saturday to crush number-two-ranked Georgia Tech 34–0 in Athens and earn a Rose Bowl berth against UCLA on New Year's Day.

Unfortunately, Sinkwich entered the final game of his college career with a pair of sprained ankles. He was forced to turn over much of the rushing load to his heir apparent, Trippi, and the sophomore responded with 27 carries for 115 yards against the Bruins. But he couldn't crack the end zone.

The game went scoreless into the fourth quarter, with 90,000 fans on hand in Pasadena. Finally, Georgia blocked a Bob Waterfield punt out of the end zone for a safety and a 2–0 lead in the fourth quarter. Later in the fourth quarter, Clyde Ehrhardt picked off a Waterfield pass and returned it to the 25-yard line.

Georgia pounded the ball in, and Sinkwich eventually got the call from the 1-yard line. Sinkwich ran it across, and Leo Costa added the PAT for a 9–0 Georgia win.

The Bulldogs were consensus national champions that year, the school's first title. Sinkwich became the first player from a southern school to win the Heisman and was the only player from the region to capture the award until LSU's Billy Cannon won it in 1959.

Sinkwich finished his career with 2,271 yards rushing, 2,331 yards passing, and 60 touchdowns—30 each on the ground and through the air. But numbers couldn't reflect the impact Sinkwich had on the program. Through his performances in high-profile games, Sinkwich forced the rest of the country to pay attention to Georgia football for the first time.

"He put us on the map," Magill said.

Sinkwich was inducted into the College Football Hall of Fame in 1954, with his achievements still fresh in the minds of the voters. Nearly 60 years after the end of Sinkwich's college career, it can be difficult to put his numbers in perspective, compared to Herschel Walker's gaudy running stats and Zeier's equally impressive passing numbers.

But an undated magazine article from the 1950s offers some insight into the importance of Sinkwich's accomplishments. The one-page story, drawing heavily on statistics, asserts that Sinkwich was in fact the best offensive player ever, superior even to the Galloping Ghost, Red Grange of Illinois. "The greatest offensive back in modern intercollegiate football—and your record book will prove it—was Frank Sinkwich of the University of Georgia," it reads.

At the end of the story is a chart of the two players' statistical totals in their three-year careers, and Grange's 4,280 yards of offense from 1923 to 1925 fell more than 300 yards short of Sinkwich's totals.

An Unfortunate Injury

Unfortunately, the end of college marked the beginning of the end of Sinkwich's greatness on the football field.

Because of his flat feet and high blood pressure, he was not accepted into the Marine Corps, so he signed with the Detroit Lions. He was an All-Pro player his first two seasons in the league and was named the league's most valuable player in 1944.

After that season, he was accepted into the Air Force and was sent to Colorado Springs. While playing on the Air Force football team there, Sinkwich suffered a serious knee injury. Two operations couldn't fix the damage, and at the age of 25, Sinkwich's career was over.

He coached for a few years, at Furman and [the University of Tampa], but he eventually gave up football altogether and came back to his adopted hometown of Athens to start a family. Sinkwich became a beer distributor in northeast Georgia and stayed one for the rest of his life.

His son, Frank Jr., still runs the Miller Lite distributorship his father used to be involved with. Frank Jr. has lived his entire life in Clarke County, attending Athens High and UGA, and while he never inherited his father's athletic ability, he shares his dad's affection for the town and the university.

"He loved athletics, he lived and breathed it," Frank Jr. said. "On Saturdays, TV was made for him to watch not just football, but all sports. He was an avid fan of everything."

As a fan, Sinkwich was a major supporter of UGA athletics for the rest of his life, and he chaired the committee to raise funds for the construction of Butts-Mehre Heritage Hall along with his mentor, Hartman. The building was completed in 1987.

Three years later, on October 22, 1990, Sinkwich died in Athens after a long battle with cancer. He was 70 years old.

Back in Youngstown, Ohio, a monument honors one of the town's favorite sons. On April 28, 1988, Chaney High School's football field was renamed Frank Sinkwich Athletic Field.

If Bill Hartman had had enough gas in his tank in 1939, that field might be named something else—maybe after Paul Something-or-Other.

"You know, that other boy, he never did play at Ohio State," Hartman said. "He went, but he never turned out."

Sinkwich, though, turned the history of Georgia football around.

Loran Smith, *Athens Banner-Herald*

TRIPPI SUCCESSFUL ON AND OFF THE FIELD

In this feature from 2003, Loran Smith gives his insight into the great Charley Trippi, the captain of the Bulldogs' 1946 undefeated and untied Sugar Bowl champion team and a member of both the College and Pro Football Halls of Fame.

In college football today, there is an abundance of talent, and with limited scholarships, it is difficult to develop a dynasty. Consistent winner, maybe, but you can pretty much forget dynasties. Obviously Mark Richt seeks to develop a consistency of championship success like he experienced at Florida State. His timing may be good, but his challenge, most would agree, is that he competes in the SEC. Georgia won three conference titles in a row with Herschel Walker from 1980 to 1982, but the closest the Bulldogs came to anything in the way of a dynasty was in the early 1940s. First, it was a 9–1–1 season in 1941 and a 40–26 dismantling of TCU in the Orange Bowl. A conference championship, Rose Bowl victory, and national championship followed in 1942. An Oil Bowl victory came in 1945, and next there was an undefeated SEC championship season in 1946, which ended with a 20–10 victory over North Carolina in the Sugar Bowl. The team won the national title. There is no telling what Wallace Butts would have put together in the way of championships had there been peace on earth.

Much of Butts's pre- and post-war success was due, in large part, to Charley Trippi.

When Trippi played, bowl games were expected. Winning a championship was pretty much a given with him in the lineup. It was a sad day when he went to the NFL.

In the mid-1950s, Trippi returned to Athens from pro football to work as backfield coach for his alma mater.

Trippi and I became friends, much to my great pleasure. I knew his legend. I knew his competitive reputation and enjoyed being around him. He was clever and delightfully cynical. He was engaging and disarming. He often took me on recruiting trips. His invitation went something like this: "Wanna go to Atlanta with me Friday night to see a game? Beer and expense-account steak?" Naturally I enjoyed his company and always thought I could learn something about football while with one of the greatest ever to play the game. And that expense-account steak was a fulfilling treat, for sure, for a kid on partial scholarship and pretty much working his way through school.

Charley even got me a job writing for a sports magazine. The piece appeared under his byline, but the good news was that I got paid $25 each month to put it together. For a long time I enjoyed kidding him about our author team. "If you could type, I would lose that $25 each month," I jokingly reminded him.

When it comes to money Trippi has always spent wisely. There is a generous side to him that many are not familiar with. But it is there, and he takes umbrage with those who wisecrack about his handling of money. A guy, well known for his tight-fisted style, once said of Trippi at a local banquet, "Trippi is the richest man in Athens. Also the cheapest." Trippi has never forgotten that. Give him credit for good money management, but don't call him cheap. He might be wisely conservative with his money, even frugal, but for sure he is not cheap.

Since those recruiting trips and expense-account steaks, I have been out to lunch and dinner with Trippi countless times. To this day, I have never picked up a check.

One of the most honored athletes ever at Georgia, Trippi gives to family, church, and local charities, but you wouldn't know about it. He believes that such things should be done privately and never talked about. That is why he doesn't appreciate people taking unwarranted shots at him at coffee clubs and banquets.

Trippi has many fine attributes, and those who played with him will tell you that they seldom played with a greater competitor. Once when I worked with a national television network as a spotter for a Bulldogs game, the color analyst was Paul Christman, who played with Trippi when they were with the old Chicago Cardinals. "I've never played with a better back than Trippi," Christman said. "He could do whatever it took. In short-yardage situations, nobody was better. When you needed a big play, he was your man."

When Trippi played there were no facemasks, which led to a cheap shot that severely damaged his face. The 49ers' John Henry Johnson, who eventually made the Hall of Fame, eased up to Trippi after a play had ended and blindsided him. Extensive plastic surgery was required to repair Trippi's jaw and nose.

There is an interesting sidelight to the Johnson episode. Years after his dastardly, dirty blow, John Henry was being interviewed for one of those ESPN memory pieces. He remarked that he owed his life to Trippi. Johnson knew that the mafia in Chicago had great affection for Italian sports heroes like Trippi and Joe DiMaggio. All Trippi had to do was to send word that Johnson needed to be taken care of and he would have wound up at the bottom of some river.

John Henry knew that and gratefully said so before the camera.

Trippi, certainly not a dirty player, could dish it out with the best. He could also take it. The battles he had with the Bears' Ed Sprinkle are legendary in Chicago. Once Trippi went up to Sprinkle, pulled off his helmet with one hand, punched him with the other, and walked off the field.

One day not long ago, I called Trippi and disguised my voice to his wife, Peggy, and told her it was Ed Sprinkle calling. Trippi became excited as she handed him the phone. "Eddie, where are you? Are you in town?"

After a slight pause, I said to Trippi, "What is going on? You were never nice to Sprinkle in Chicago."

"That is all in the past," Trippi laughed. "We're friends now. We play golf together at NFL outings." There is a message here. You fight it out on the field, no holds barred, but become civil afterward.

Growing up in Wilkes-Barre, Pennsylvania, life was a challenge for Trippi and his family. His dad, Joseph, was an anthracite coal miner, and had it not been for football, chances are that Trippi would have taken up employment residency in the mines. He wanted a better life, but he respected men like his father who labored for their families.

Even today, one of his proudest possessions is a trophy he received from his hometown for being named Athlete of the Century a few years ago. It is made of anthracite and is prominently displayed in his home. You won't, however, find a big collection of trophies elsewhere.

Trippi does have scrapbooks but never for display. The only reason for the scrapbooks is that he wants his career to be remembered for his children and grandchildren.

In his formative years in Pittston, Pennsylvania, Trippi wore overalls. He had two pair. One for school and one for play. He would have gotten a serious whipping if had played in his school overalls.

He owned only one pair of shoes, which meant that when he wanted to go out for football, he could not afford to buy any cleats for competition.

His father told him that the family had no money to buy football shoes.

"You got no business playing football," his father said. "You'll get your leg broke. And when you do, I'll break the other one."

One day on the school playground Trippi, who had borrowed a football, started booming punts in his street shoes which got the attention of Coach Paul Shelby at Pittston High. Shelby immediately invited Trippi to football practice, but Trippi told the coach that he didn't have any shoes.

Shelby took care of that, and the next fall Trippi became the team's number-one punter. He was also the starting center, except in punt formation. There are many who would suggest Trippi was good enough to snap the ball, run and get it, and blast off a punt before the defense could collar him.

In fact, in his first season, a low snap resulted in Trippi chasing down the bounding ball. He then zigzagged his way for an 80-yard touchdown, which put him in the backfield to stay.

A fortuitous development took place in Trippi's junior year at Pittston. He got to know a former Bulldogs football player, Harold "War Eagle" Ketron, who owned the Coca-Cola Bottling Co. in nearby Wilkes-Barre.

Ketron gave Trippi part-time jobs and later sent him to La Salle Academy on Long Island. At Pittston the college scouts didn't pay Trippi all that much attention, but after a sensational prep career, everybody wanted to sign him to a college scholarship.

One of the things Trippi learned, other than hard work, from his daddy was to keep his word. When the scouts started coming around, Trippi told them he was not interested for one simple reason: "I had given my word to Mr. Ketron that I would sign with Georgia."

Trippi was a remarkable halfback at Georgia and later in the NFL. His slick ability to evade tacklers made him one of the most competent runners in college and pro football. On top of that, he punted and handled kicks throughout his career.

In his prime with the old Chicago Cardinals, the legendary Jim Thorpe was watching Trippi play one Sunday and said, "He is the greatest football player I have ever seen."

Bobby Dodd, longtime coach at Georgia Tech, said Trippi was the greatest safetyman ever. Dodd further stated that because of Trippi's offensive ability Trippi was the best all-around football player he ever saw.

It was Bill Hartman who suggested to Butts that it would be overwhelming for defenses to put Trippi and Frank Sinkwich in the backfield at the same time.

In late 1942, Hartman, who had been backfield coach prior to his military duty, was stationed in Atlanta. This enabled him to scout Georgia Tech, the Bulldogs' main opponent, on weekends. He would consult with Butts and the staff and had an occasional opportunity to meet with them.

He recommended to Butts that it would enhance an already explosive offense if the Bulldogs lined up with Sinkwich at fullback and Trippi at tailback. At the start of the season Sinkwich was the starter at tailback and Trippi backed him up.

Hartman reasoned, along with Butts, that Sinkwich was more of an inside threat, while Trippi's skills made him dangerously proficient at plays to the outside.

"We were using the single wing," Hartman said. "With Sinkwich at fullback, he had many productive options with his ability at that position. Harvard, which still had a viable football program nationally, had developed the spin series, where their fullback would spin as he went into the line and developed a variety of plays off the spin. We had a number of those plays, and we had a number involving the half spin.

"Sinkwich was a natural at spin plays. With his remarkable quickness, he could explode past the line of scrimmage on traps. He was so good on inside plays. Against Tech in 1942 he made a half spin and handed off to Trippi going wide, and Charley went 80 yards for a touchdown.

"We would have had the two of them in the backfield for the Rose Bowl, but Sinkwich had two sprained ankles and could not play very much."

Sinkwich did get into the game and scored Georgia's only touchdown, in a 9–0 victory, from the 1-yard line. It was a big day for Trippi, who rushed 27 times for 115 yards and received the Helms Award as the game's outstanding player. Trippi has been named to the Rose Bowl's all-time team as a halfback.

A member of both the College and Pro Football Halls of Fame, Trippi, following his junior season in 1945, could have turned pro, but Coach Butts wanted to make sure there would be no problem with him playing for the Bulldogs in 1946. Following the Tech game in 1945, Butts announced, in an emotional scene in the locker room, that Trippi would be team captain next year. A teammate, John Donaldson, remembers well that scene. "We all appreciated Charley," Donaldson said, "and we were pleased that Coach Butts wanted him to return. We knew what Trippi could do, and we wanted him to be with us in 1946. I was his teammate; I respected him and wanted him to stay. I think most of the team felt that if he came back, we could have a great year, and that is exactly what happened."

After returning to Athens from the NFL in 1958, Trippi coached the Bulldogs backs until 1963, when he returned to the Cardinals to coach the running backs.

When Trippi left, he knew he would return to Athens after a few seasons coaching with the pros. Athens had become home, and he had accumulated considerable interests in real estate.

Trippi always had excellent real-estate instincts, and he had money to invest in the 1950s and 1960s. After his playing career at Georgia had ended, he signed a $100,000 contract with the Cardinals. On top of that, Earl Mann of the Atlanta Crackers paid Trippi $10,000 to play a season of minor league baseball. After the Crackers' season ended, Trippi reported to the Cardinals in 1947, and St. Louis won the NFL championship.

Trippi, who believes he could have made it in big-league baseball, had no interest in playing two sports. "It would not have been fair to either team," he says.

And that is something Trippi always had, something that many of these Johnny-come-lately superstars seem not to have—loyalty to the team. Trippi never put himself ahead of the team and his teammates.

Jim Klobuchar and Fran Tarkenton, *Tarkenton*

THE QUARTERBACK

In this chapter from his autobiography, Tarkenton, *the All-American quarterback looks back on his collegiate career, which included an SEC championship and Orange Bowl victory in 1959.*

When I came back to Georgia after my first year in professional football and my exposure to people like the Dutchman, Ray Nitschke, and Alex Karras, people said, "My, that must have been a shock going into that world from the University of Georgia." I'm just not so sure it was all that shocking. My life at Georgia had just as much suspense. It had almost as many hazards. It certainly had the full quota of characters.

I wasn't generally heralded as the football messiah at Georgia, because I played high school ball in the same town, Athens. The townspeople had theories about that. Athens kids weren't supposed to get a fair shake at Georgia because they were fully exposed, week in and week out, to the Georgia staff, and everybody was conscious of their limitations. It was the kind of theory that had something in common with many theories: it was really pretty hard to prove, and it was probably filled with gas.

I don't know how I could have been better programmed for a high school career. By the time my family left Washington, D.C., and came to Athens, where Daddy was going to preach, I had decided without equivocation that I was going to be a professional athlete. I fantasized with bubblegum picture games in the attic, and I fantasized in the sandlots. I played all the time. I was bigger than the other kids my age, and I tended to dominate the ballgames. I don't blush to say I had big feet. Somebody started calling me "Foots." Why not?

At the age of 13 I was 5'10", weighed 145 pounds, and wore a size 10½ shoe. Today I'm 6' and wear an 11 shoe. The way my feet developed early, some guy said I was wasting my time trying to be an athlete and should grow up to be a detective.

But Athens was great for kid ball, and I played everything. In high school football we had a coach named Weyman Sellers, who was notorious. He wrote the book on how to be a tough football coach and is known in southern football almost as well as Bear Bryant is. If you lost a ballgame Friday night, Weyman Sellers was the kind of coach who would bring you back on the field Saturday morning and scrimmage you for four hours. At practices we would run a mile, take our exercises, run 10 50-yard wind sprints, and then start playing football. It was incredible. When I was introduced to the Dutchman's two-a-day drills at the Vikings camp in Bemidji [State University], everybody seemed appalled. They could never figure out why I was so calm about it. Actually I was grateful. If Sellers ran the Vikings he would have scheduled a third [practice] at night. But he taught me the fundamentals of playing quarterback, the techniques that stood up for the rest of my career. He was relentless about teaching the quarterback to make the right moves taking the ball, handling it, handing off. Most of what I still use I got from the Athens High School Trojans and Weyman Sellers.

It's still probably the best thing I do as a quarterback, handle the ball, which is an acknowledgment I know John Unitas will be pleased to hear. But in my junior year at Athens something traumatic happened. I got a bad shoulder separation and just couldn't throw the ball for more than 15 to 20 yards. But we had a great team and killed everybody. I quarterbacked, ran, and tried to sound inspirational. We got into the state championship against Valdosta, which was the Massillon, Ohio, of Georgia football. I ran a kickoff back 99 yards and threw one pass the whole game. It was incomplete. We won, 41–20, and please don't draw any conclusions.

Because we moved up in classification and we lost some fine players, we didn't do much my senior season, but the colleges seemed interested in me. I couldn't think of a better place to become a football hero than the University of Georgia, which already had two quarterbacks who aspired to that status, Charlie Britt and Tommy Lewis. Although younger and respectful, I decided it was just a matter of time until I would take over. One of the people who didn't necessarily agree with this logic was the head coach, Wally Butts.

Coach Butts was the first in a long line of brilliant football minds who didn't think that Francis Tarkenton had much of a future as a professional football player. At the time, though, Butts thought I had a reasonable chance of lettering at Georgia, eventually. Our timetables just happened to disagree.

Coach Butts was really far ahead of his time in his approach to football tactics. He was a pugnacious little guy who could talk like a carny worker on the practice field and lead us in prayer the next day. We always had a devotional before the game, of course. It was part of the southern tradition, and the coach was a churchgoer who came from a Baptist college, Mercer. He also conducted a prayer session afterward, unless we lost.

Another thing we did before the game once in a while was to go over the opposition's game plan—if it happened to fall into our hands. We were in the midst of this quiet, contemplative period on a Saturday, listening to soft background music of University of Georgia fight songs and alma mater anthems and trying to feel very fierce about facing Vanderbilt in a couple of hours. Coach Butts called me in and explained that some bellhop at the hotel where Vanderbilt was staying had "stumbled into" the Vanderbilt game plan. By the rankest coincidence we now had it. It told all about how Vanderbilt was going to use the monsterman on defense and what stuff they were going to use against our passing game. All of that and more. I figured they must know what they're doing, I mean our board of strategy, so I just filed away the information. I don't think we called our agents "plumbers" in those days. And I'm sure the bellhop just didn't flat-out steal that game plan. I have no idea how he came into possession of it, and I'm also mortally sure that most teams in the Southeastern Conference had some version of this intelligence system. We did beat the daylights out of Vanderbilt that year.

The guy who really got me ready psychologically and technically for college football was a man named Quinton Lumpkin, the freshman coach at the University of Georgia. He had been a great center at Georgia. He was the kind who lived in the dormitory with the players, a principled, hard-fibered, decent guy who was a man among men. Nobody ever challenged Quinton Lumpkin. He was tough, all right, but a gentle guy at the core, a man you could confide in if things got rough. We played three freshman games and won them all, and two weeks before the varsity's opening game, we beat the varsity.

As a sophomore, I naturally began as the third-string quarterback behind Charlie Britt and Tommy Lewis. Charlie later played defensive back in the pros and was a teammate of mine for a while with the Vikings in the mid-1960s. Until Terry Bradshaw, I never saw a quarterback with Britt's physical qualifications. He was 6'2", had a powerful arm, and ran like a deer. Tommy Lewis was a tremendous passer, too. And then there was Tarkenton, with the kind of arm you can define any way you want. In the face of this, I still thought I would be the starting Georgia quarterback in a couple of weeks. I really didn't look on that as bravado. I actually thought I had enough to give the team.

We opened at Texas, and I watched most of the game from the bench. I don't think we made a first down the first three quarters.

I was standing next to Wally Butts, convinced the Georgia coaching staff had decided to redshirt me, hold me out of competition my sophomore season. To hell with that noise. I started telling Coach Butts, "I can do it, I can get you a touchdown in this game, I can get this thing going." I still hadn't regained the full strength in my right arm in the two years since my shoulder separation, but I could throw adequately.

In the last quarter, Texas punted the ball down to our 5. Before Butts could haul me back, I was running out to the huddle. Somehow the University of Georgia football team went 95 yards with Francis Tarkenton at quarterback on his first series. To compound the absurdity of it, he passed for the touchdown. He also passed for the two-point conversion, and Georgia led, 8–7.

Texas had a bunch of strong runners, though, people like Walt Fondren. So they went the length of the field to score, and we had four minutes left. I was poised on the sideline, the adrenaline oozing. And what does Coach Butts tell me? He says Charlie Britt is going in there to win the game.

I have never really been able to persuade many people right out of the blocks—I mean, for the first five or 10 years they have watched me play—that I belonged in the front row in football. My high school team obliterated everybody in sight in my junior year, and as a senior I played very well, yet I never made the first-team all-state team. In basketball I made it as a freshman. But not in football. The number of nonbelievers in Francis Tarkenton in football has been very impressive, and you might even say scary. This might make it easier to understand why Coach Butts went immediately to Charlie Britt after I took the team 95 yards in the fourth quarter. Butts was looking to play the big, strong quarterback. Charlie tried his damnedest, but we lost.

You can imagine the reaction in Athens. I was an instant martyr. They thought Butts was crazy, and they thought the old proverb about Athens boys getting screwed at the University of Georgia surely had been confirmed. The next week they practically passed a town ordinance demanding that Tarkenton should start the second game.

Coach Butts was no greenhorn as a politician. He read the polls shrewdly. He decided an excellent choice for his starting quarterback the next game would be the sophomore from Athens. I quarterbacked the first three plays of the game. Butts then substituted Charlie Britt, who played the rest of the game, which we lost.

In the next two or three weeks I got in once in a while, but on one particular Saturday I was something less than the next Sammy Baugh. In practice the following Monday, Butts gave me the full barrage—language I just didn't think a coach was capable of using on a football player. Some really awful stuff. I was the child of a fundamentalist church, you should remember, and even *hell* and *damn* were foreign to me then. Here was my head coach calling me names I had only seen on the washroom walls. I knew Butts's reputation as a slaughterhouse orator when he was chewing out a player, but this was the first time it had happened to me, and it wasn't going to happen again. I was finished with Georgia, and I walked off the field.

I met with Butts that night, and I told him I wasn't coming back because I didn't have to accept his kind of abuse. He tried to talk me out of it. I said my mind was set. One of my teammates, Pat Guy, felt as strongly as I did about dehumanizing coaching tirades. Another was

Phil Ash, who lived in Stone Mountain, a town a few miles east of Atlanta. The three of us took off together. I think Phil was pretty much along for the ride, but we spent the night in his home, planning to enroll at Florida State and leave the Bulldogs and Wallace Butts far behind.

The next day, we had a visit from Quinton Lumpkin, the only coach in the world we would have listened to under the circumstances. He just walked in quietly and sort of sat around, talking a little about hunting and fishing. We told him about our intentions.

He said he understood all that, and how things happen the way they did on the practice field, but Georgia really needed us, and our teammates needed us, and none of the strong words spoken by Coach Butts were in any way personal. He would guarantee that. I think Quinton Lumpkin meant every word he said, because it never occurred to me then, and never will, that this man might be capable of saying something he didn't believe. Naturally, we went back to Athens.

From then on I quarterbacked a lot, and Charlie Britt played defense primarily, and a first-rate defense at that. We started winning. In my junior year Britt would start at quarterback and then shift to defense. I'd come in on offense in the first quarter and quarterback the rest of the game. I'm not sure how Wally Butts arrived at this formula, but it worked.

We were selected to finish 10th in the Southeastern Conference that year, 1959, and when you examined the rosters of the other teams it was not hard to understand why. Louisiana State had people like Billy Cannon, Johnny Robinson, and Warren Rabb; Mississippi had Charlie Flowers and Jake Gibbs. Jackie Burkett and Zeke Smith and a half-dozen other outstanding players were at Auburn. But we opened the season by beating Alabama, and when we went into the ninth week, it was Georgia and Auburn for the championship and the Orange Bowl. The finish was the kind you wouldn't have believed if you saw it in the old Monogram movies. It was tied, 7–7, and Bobby Walden went back to punt: the one, the only Bobby Walden who starred for the Cairo, Georgia, Syrupmakers—my teammate later with the Vikings, and now annually picking up Super Bowl checks with the Steelers. Bobby lined up to kick, and Charlie Britt, who was then in at quarterback, was the blocking back. I think Charlie dropped back a little deep, because Bobby delivered a terrific effort and kicked the ball right into Charlie's rear end. In front of 60,000 people. I never saw a guy look more shocked in all my life.

I don't mean Charlie. I mean Bobby.

Auburn revived before either one of them did and recovered the ball on our 1. When they scored it was 13–7. The game wound down to a minute and a half left. We recovered a fumble on their 45, and I threw three straight passes, incomplete. On fourth-and-10 I hit one. We reached the Auburn 7, but they snarled up a screen pass, and with 30 seconds left we're on the 13-yard line, fourth down.

It was a huge game—for the championship, the honor of Georgia, Coach Butts, and all of the good, great Baptists. The whole South was tuned in. I called a timeout but did not go to the sideline to visit Coach Butts. We just didn't have any plays programmed for fourth-and-13 with 30 seconds to go and the whole reborn Confederacy hanging on the outcome. I drew up a play in the huddle.

I actually did, just like the John R. Tunis books I grew up with. We didn't have split ends in those days. The two pass-catching ends were always lined up tight, and there were the conventional three running backs in the backfield. Essentially the play was a quarterback rollout to the right in which everything would flow right, the blocking and the receivers, except for the left end, a fellow named Bill Herron. I told him to stay in and block, and count, "One thousand one, one thousand two, one thousand three, one thousand four." When he finished the count I wanted him to sprint into the left corner of the end zone.

We got the play going and I rolled right. I was dying to see what was happening with our left end. I wanted to look back, but I made myself carry out the deception. The whole stadium was looking at the rightward flow of the play, and all I could do was pray that the Auburn secondary was just as attentive. When I finished my own "one thousand four," I stopped and pivoted for a look at where Bill Herron was supposed to be. And Lord have mercy, there he was, wide open.

I ripped it crossfield, scared to death he was either going to drop it or the ball was going into the stands. Neither happened. We had the touchdown. Durwood Pennington kicked the extra point, and Georgia was in the Orange Bowl. I almost never call plays like that in the NFL, and I don't usually admit it when I do. Unprofessional. The computer has a play for every contingency. Except not quite, and the computers don't have to explain it all to the fans after the ballgame.

We beat Dan Devine's Missouri team, 14–0, in the Orange Bowl that year. And the next season, my senior year at Georgia, was presentable. So I decided the world was now ready to bestow its rewards on Francis Tarkenton. Elaine and I were married at the end of the season. We had met three years before at a fraternity party when we were both freshmen. My date was her roommate, but it didn't take me long to rearrange the pairings, making myself quickly unpopular with my date and Elaine's in the process. Elaine was the kind of girl who made you stop surveying. She was—and is—a beautiful, dark-haired woman with stunning blue eyes and a brightness of personality and mind. She was a majorette, but the band played for varsity games and she had no knowledge whatsoever of the freshman quarterback. I thought I might help familiarize her. I asked her to church services the next morning, and we were a twosome thereafter. She enjoyed my playing football in college, but she was never overwhelmed by it. So she needled me more than somewhat when we went directly from our wedding night to the practice camp for the annual Blue-Gray game after the 1960 season. She said the romanticists would be horrified.

We became close friends of the Norman Sneads at the Blue-Gray game. Both of us were waiting on word from the NFL draft. Snead's Wake Forest team was 1–9 for the 1960 season, but he was a big guy with a cannon arm, and it was generally assumed he would go in the first round. I don't know what was generally assumed about Francis Tarkenton. I was assuming he would be picked in the first round.

The team I wanted to draft me, of course, was the Washington Redskins. They were having organizational problems, but Washington was the city of my boyhood excitements and where I had built up my own Hall of Fame invincibles—the Sammy Baughs in football and the Bones McKinneys in basketball. When Daddy had to take the family out of the city and move South, I had made this very solemn personal pledge to the nation's capital that I would return. I don't think Douglas MacArthur could have made such a vow more significantly.

Like any other pending draft choice, I had been getting letters and telephone calls. One of the calls came from a man named Billy Bye. I later found him to be a very companionable fellow. He was a former star of the University of Minnesota, a high school coach, and for a couple of years a member of the Vikings organization. Bye introduced himself and said he represented the Vikings: I had never heard of the Vikings. They sounded like an eight-man team playing in northern Georgia. But Bye said they were a new franchise in pro football.

I still didn't connect the Vikings as an expansion team in the National Football League. I thought they might be in one of the minor leagues, like the Bethlehem Steelers. But Bye said they would be playing in the National Football League in 1961, and would I be interested in playing for them if I were drafted? I said, "Well, sure, I'd be glad to consider the Vikings." But privately I'd rather not, because Washington was where I wanted to go, not with the Vikings or the new American Football League, but back to the Potomac. I was even prepared to row a football over the river if that's what it took.

The Washington Redskins drafted Norman Snead on the first round. I was deflated. Just smothered. I then waited for the news report or the telephone call that would identify the NFL team that had drafted Tarkenton on the first round.

Nothing showed.

I thought the wires must be down. I had been fully impregnated by the quarterback syndrome of the time. All the first-rate college quarterbacks, the ones with any prestige and promise as professionals, were automatic first-round choices. I was not a first-round choice. I wasn't picked in the second round either. Finally, I received a telephone call from Bert Rose, the Vikings general manager. He informed me I had the distinction of being drafted in the third round by the Minnesota Vikings, and that I could expect a visit shortly from their traveling agent, Joe Thomas.

I think my end of the conversation was courteous, but brief. Thomas did materialize in a day or so, followed by Ed McKeever, representing Boston—now New England—of the AFL. Both of them were likable and talked straight. Thomas offered a figure he thought was generous but within the Vikings' means, a package of about $15,000. McKeever was prepared to pay me $17,500 in salary and $5,000 in bonus to sign with Boston. I had to tell him the National Football League was my idea of the zenith in athletics, and I would therefore sign with the Vikings.

I think the exact figure the Vikings offered was $12,500 in salary and $3,500 in bonus, which the accountants tell me is about what I now make in one game. But at the time my un-toppable goal was to make $20,000 in one season. If I could do that, I told myself, I would have achieved everything in pro football within my capabilities and visions.

I asked Joe Thomas who the Vikings coach was. He said the coach hadn't been selected yet. But when he was, it was sure to be a choice who would enrich my career as a pro football player. Joe said the new coach would be a man I would spend many hours of warm society with. [In actuality, the new coach was Norm Van Brocklin, with whom Tarkenton would have a stormy relationship.]

Henry Leifermann, *The New York Times*

HERSCHEL WALKER'S RUN TO GLORY

By his sophomore season, Herschel Walker had already captured the nation's attention. In November 1981, a season after setting the all-time NCAA freshman rushing record and a year before winning the Heisman, Walker was the subject of this penetrating feature story in The New York Times Magazine.

In the spring of 1980, Herschel Walker was a black teenager in the mid-Georgia town of Wrightsville (population, 2,350). Walker was not just the star of the Johnson County High School football team. He was the most sought-after high school player in the country.

College recruiters flew into Wrightsville by helicopter, some staying months, wooing Walker. One, from the University of Georgia, lived in a house lent him by a wealthy white alumnus of Georgia, and it was Georgia, to the regret of hundreds of other colleges, that Herschel Walker chose to attend.

Now, less than two years later, Walker is already one of college football's most awesome running backs—not only today, some say ever—and fans around the country may catch a glimpse of his superb running style if the Georgia-Florida game next Saturday is nationally televised, as it seems likely to be. In his debut season, in which he broke the freshman rushing record set by Tony Dorsett (now with the Dallas Cowboys) at the University of Pittsburgh, he was the first freshman to finish as high as third in the voting for the Heisman Memorial Trophy, given to college football's best athlete, and he was also the first freshman ever to make the Football Writers' All-American team.

This year, Walker has been even better. Opponents know he's coming now but still cannot stop him. In the final seconds of Georgia's 37–7 victory over Mississippi, it was the Ole Miss fans who chanted, "Herschel, Herschel, Herschel." Walker gained 265 yards in that game and scored a touchdown by diving over the line of scrimmage, landing on one hand, and springing into the end zone like an acrobat. Mississippi coach Steve Sloan said afterward, "There's only so much you can do. It's a good thing we played an eight-man front." When Georgia beat Vanderbilt, 53–21, Walker broke the Georgia career rushing record in half the time it had taken to set the old one.

Gil Brandt, vice president and director of player personnel for the Dallas Cowboys and generally considered the leading scout of the National Football League, says Herschel Walker and Houston Oilers running back Earl Campbell are the only players he has seen who could have gone directly from high school to the NFL. Tom Braatz, player personnel director for the Atlanta Falcons, says Walker would have been everyone's number-one draft choice.

This year, Walker may become the first sophomore to win the Heisman Trophy. If Walker comes through as a pro as did many recent Heisman winners, he will have left another set of giant footsteps for future running backs to follow. Such a future, of course, is predicated on Walker's staying reasonably intact. Because there is always the chance of a college football player sustaining a disabling injury, Herschel Walker's name not only appears today on stadium programs and sports pages, but on a million-dollar insurance policy with Lloyd's of London, for which his family pays the annual premium of approximately $12,000.

William Sutton of Toronto, a Lloyd's representative who has written more than 1,000 similar policies for professional and college athletes, believes that Walker is the first college football player to so insure himself. Therefore, according to Sutton, there is no body of statistics from which to calculate the odds of a player becoming injured. In figuring the premium against the amount of the insurance, Lloyd's has estimated that one and a quarter college football players out of every 100 will sustain a career-ending injury each season. Herschel Walker's problem is to avoid becoming one of those one and a quarter players.

At the University of Georgia—where past football heroes have usually been white, where about half the present football team is black, with only one black coach out of 14, and where the student body remains largely white—Walker is an unaccustomed sort of campus hero. Beyond the usual idolization of a football star at a big-time football school, there is an extra measure of curiosity about Walker, not least from white women students.

On the practice field, he looks indestructible. At 19, he dwarfs most of his teammates, muscles layered in great slabs and chunks, rump-size thighs, tight 31-inch waist, chest and shoulders of a bull, 6'2", and 220 pounds. He seems even bigger on one of the infrequent occasions when he loses his temper. Recently, for instance, during a practice scrimmage, a defensive back piled onto him late after a gang-tackle had carried him out of bounds. Walker's elbow, driving up and back, just missed taking the defensive back's head off.

Vince Dooley, Georgia's head coach, said that explosive, angry moment was the first of its kind he had ever seen from Walker. Asked about the incident later, Walker said, "It was my fault. I relaxed when I was out of bounds, and that's when the hit came. You just don't relax when you're carrying the ball."

He has been controlling himself, with only a few slips, since Wrightsville. When he became a football star, some of the town's richest whites showed him deference while other blacks were being beaten by white mobs at the courthouse, and while most blacks in town were simply poor and quiet. Herschel Walker kept his feelings to himself—about the segregated school he attended until he was eight, about never getting to go swimming, and about not being invited to the country club banquet celebrating the state football championship to which he led his high school team.

Sleeping only a few hours a night since junior high, this loner often drives around before dawn in the college town of Athens in the $12,000 black Trans Am his parents gave him. (Walker and his family refuse to comment on how they financed the car last year or the insurance premiums this year. Usually, however, a player of Walker's stature or his family can get a loan and pay only the interest; the principal is refinanced until a professional contract is signed. If this were the case, though, a spokesman for the National Collegiate Athletic Association's enforcement division said that it would be against its regulations. The spokesman added that if the family's house were used as collateral, that would abide by NCAA rules.)

When Walker does socialize, campus gossip has it that he does so more with whites than blacks, a racist accusation to some, to which Walker responds, "Well, mostly I hang out with the football team." It is also said he is not the quiet, reasonable, hardworking young man he presents himself to be, but a teenage, black Svengali coolly calculating plans for fame and fortune ever since high school. One thing on which there is no disagreement is his ability to move the ball.

No one in college or professional football recalls such a combination of size, strength, and speed as Herschel Walker's. The speed, almost Olympic-dash caliber, is unique: he reaches full speed after his first step and can move 10 yards during the next second in full uniform. In a track suit, looking twice the size of anyone else in the starting blocks, Walker is faster, coming within 0.27 seconds of the world indoor record for the 60-yard dash, and he would like to try for a gold medal in the 1984 Olympics. Walker is almost as fast, on the start and over 100 yards, as Bob Hayes, the legendary Olympic track star and former wide receiver for Dallas, one of the fastest men ever to play pro football. There is simply no way to measure the kinetic energy released, the impact endured, in stopping someone that big moving that fast. In high school, Walker simply ran over tacklers, then outran the pursuit.

Not surprisingly, Herschel Walker's first collegiate touchdown became a legend. On opening day against Tennessee last year, Dooley listed Walker as third-string tailback. He had two tailbacks to test ahead of Walker. When Dooley at last sent in the nation's most-recruited freshman, Tennessee led, 15–0. "The first two times he carried," Dooley recalls, "he gained only two and eight yards. He didn't know where he was running. I didn't know, and neither did Tennessee. But he was running. He was taking off somewhere."

In the third quarter, on the Tennessee 16, Walker took a pitch and began a power sweep right. He was over the line of scrimmage and reversing field, cutting left, in perhaps two seconds. Six tacklers got a hand or two on Walker within those few yards, but he broke away from them all, leaving a defensive end flat on his back as Walker approached the safety man. Walker looked neither left nor right, simply ran into him and knocked him flat, leaving a cleat mark on the chest of his jersey and racing between two Tennessee cornerbacks for Georgia's first touchdown of the season.

Walker scored later, Georgia won, 16–15, and the 16-yard run electrified his teammates. The rest of the season went the same way for Walker: three touchdowns—one a 76-yard run—against Texas A&M the next week, then four games in which he gained more than 200 yards each. Walker's running—simply how he went from one place to another while carrying the football—came under extraordinary dissection. "When a hole closes," wrote one analyst, "most good runners slide off or stutter-step as they seek somewhere else to go. Walker cuts away at full speed, a natural ability that cannot be taught and often cannot be stopped." Another wrote that Walker, when confronted with tacklers, can "accelerate right then and there and whip into a gear unbeknownst to mere football players."

This year, Walker told reporters a few days before Georgia's opener in Athens against Tennessee that he was "bigger, stronger, quicker, faster, and more powerful" than last season.

That Saturday afternoon, Walker played about three quarters, scored Georgia's first touchdown of the season, gained 161 yards, and ran the ball 30 times, including one run on which he left two Tennessee tacklers momentarily unconscious on the field. Georgia won, 44–0, and probably did not need Walker to win. After the game, Johnny Majors, the Tennessee head coach who had coached 1976 Heisman winner Tony Dorsett at the University of Pittsburgh, talked about Walker: "That running back is something God puts on this earth every several decades or so. He has more power, speed, and strength than anyone I've ever seen. He's got more going for him than any player that's ever played this game."

Even when Georgia lost the first game in its past 16—in September to Clemson, 13–3—and Walker had the first bad day of his career, he gained 111 yards, all but 11 of Georgia's yards rushing. The next weekend, Georgia whipped South Carolina, 24–0. Steve Sloan, the Mississippi coach, said his Rebels considered leasing a truck to prepare for their game with Georgia: "We feel this would effectively simulate Herschel Walker for our defense."

Vince Dooley, who has been at Georgia 18 years, says of the most talented athlete he may ever coach, "You learn so much on your own in this game, particularly at that position, just by doing it. He's got a chance to be one of the great backs in history if he stays healthy, if he keeps having a good supporting cast, and if his attitude keeps up."

"I just take it one day at a time," Walker says. "I'll see what happens next."

He missed 10 quarters last season with minor injuries—and still set records. In the Sugar Bowl, Walker's freshman season ended with another legend. On his second carry of the game, Walker took a crackling hit and his left shoulder was dislocated. He walked off the Superdome turf in New Orleans with one arm dangling. On the sideline, Walker told the team physician to push and pop the arm back in place. Most players are out for weeks with such an injury, but Walker returned to the field. Walker could not raise both arms to catch a pass, could not stiff-arm, and could hold the ball only with his right hand. But one arm was enough: Walker ran 36 times, gained 150 yards, and scored two touchdowns, leading Georgia to a 17–10 victory against Notre Dame and its first national championship. Without Walker's rushing that day, the Bulldogs' offensive team total would have been minus 23 yards.

Walker-watchers have noted, however, that once dislocated, that left shoulder may require less of a blow to pop it next time. In high school, he took a hit to the right shoulder and has not since been able to pass the ball in an arc.

This possibility of further injury figures in widespread speculation that Herschel Walker might try to turn pro at the end of this season— if he wins the Heisman Trophy. "It takes me a long time to make a decision," he says. "This is no make-believe world. You're going to have to answer for your errors. That's why I wait until the last minute." The NFL's rules prohibit signing underclassmen, as do the rules of the National Collegiate Athletic Association, the governing body of college sports. "What you have is a dictatorship," Walker says, "and they are telling you everything. But if you don't want to be an amateur and want to be a professional, you should have that right."

The National Basketball Association and the NCAA had similar rules until 1971, when the NBA hardship draft exempted underclassmen with financial need. Even that restriction ended, as did the hardship draft, in 1976 in a federal court settlement permitting any underclassman to sign with an NBA team. If Walker goes to court and wins, he probably would sign the richest contract in pro football history.

(Walker reportedly received a lucrative offer from the Montreal Alouettes of the Canadian Football League earlier this year, after his freshman campaign, but he decided to turn down the money, saying, "I was born in America, and it does not seem right to leave the country to play professional football.")

Herschel Walker became a loner by the third grade, says his mother, Christine Walker: "I told him to don't ever try to carry anything by yourself. He'd just say, 'Ain't nothing bothering me.' When he was sick, he wouldn't complain. I guess I'm that way some. Although I have good friends, it's not that close. He's the same. There's just not one person you confide everything in, not for us."

In this, Herschel and his mother only went one step beyond the attitude of most blacks around most whites in Johnson County: keep quiet, tell them what they want to hear, and take care of yourself.

It was not until his junior year in high school, just three years ago, that Walker became a town hero, the only black in the history of Wrightsville to be taken under the wing of such prominent local whites and wealthy Georgia boosters as Bob Newsome, a car dealer, and Ralph Jackson, a farmer.

Christine and Willis Walker started off picking cotton and raising seven children. The tin-roofed tenant farmer's house they first lived in now is used to store hay. By the time Herschel was in the eighth grade, his parents had worked their way into a white clapboard, single-story home on a hill down the road. Willis Walker worked double shifts at a kaolin plant nearby, and his wife became a supervisor at one of the garment plants built in Wrightsville during the 1970s. Herschel was the short, chubby Walker child, nothing like his older brothers, Willis Jr., now 25, and Renneth, now 24. "He was a runt," Mrs. Walker recalls.

Johnson County was forced to desegregate its schools in 1970, in time for both older Walker boys to take advantage of the athletic programs, both becoming football stars. Young Herschel wanted to be like them.

In the ninth grade, the little fat boy started growing. Then, and now, his principal diet consisted of Snickers candy bars, hamburgers, and Gatorade. (Walker alternated between the practice field and the dentist's chair for several weeks before this season began.) He weighed more than 200 pounds when he was a high school junior, and he simply ran all over the other boys.

Most people who know Herschel believe he willed himself into his current condition. His high school track coach, Tom Jordan, puts it this way: "I once told him that he needed to work on his distance endurance. A few days later, I happened to call over there, and his mother said he was out running five miles after supper. And this was on a day when we'd done 440-yard intervals, a tough day." His last year in high school, Walker won the dash and shot put events, leading his school to the state track title as well as the football championship.

But something else happened in Wrightsville during 1980, Herschel Walker's senior year: the ugliest, most violent racial conflicts in his hometown's history.

There is not a single public park, playground, or swimming pool in Wrightsville. White children can swim at the country club or at the American Legion Club, where the all-white boys' baseball team plays. For months during 1980, black demonstrators made weekly marches to the courthouse square. They wanted more blacks hired by city and county government, as well as improved private employment opportunities, and they wanted sewers repaired and roads paved in their neighborhoods.

One night, a mob of white toughs with clubs attacked the marchers, who later filed a class-action civil law suit in federal district court alleging that Sheriff Roland Attaway and other local white officials joined in the attack. On another night, Sheriff Attaway and his deputies swept through the black neighborhood, arresting 38 black men and women, all of whom he later cleared without charges. On still another evening, a black girl was hit in the neck when a white man blasted her family's trailer with a shotgun fired from a passing pickup truck. At the high school one day, six black boys jerked a jacket over a white boy's head so he could not identify them, then beat him. At one point, a few hundred state troopers were in town in case a riot developed, and at very many points through these months, Herschel Walker was asked to join. Like the majority of blacks in the county, which is about 40 percent black, Walker never did.

There were a few times after the Friday night football games when some of the protest leaders grabbed Walker, still in uniform and pads, and demanded he join them. Sheriff Attaway offered to let Herschel carry a pistol. Most of the black athletes quit the track team the same spring Herschel led it to its title.

Walker says now that he refused to join the marches because "I was too young. I was always in and out of town for track meets, and I didn't want to get involved in something I didn't know much about. I was sent to school to get a good education and learn as much in life as I can. I didn't think that was part of school."

Walker knew then that his days in Wrightsville were few to go, and he had decided he had his role in life, and Wrightsville had its. "I see myself as a poor black child from the country," he says. "I know where I come from, but I don't mind saying I want to make something out of myself." What of the economic and social condition of Wrightsville blacks? "Mostly, I just know about my family. I never checked into it."

Where did you go swimming in Wrightsville? "I didn't, I never had a chance to there," he says, without further comment.

The white adulation Walker received in Wrightsville was a prologue for what was to come in Athens. His kind of football, at least momentarily, transcends race in Georgia. Olympic sprinter Mel Lattany, a black who is a teammate of Walker's on the Georgia track team, says the only complaints he has heard on campus come from black women: "There has been a lot of discussion by black women that Herschel is white-oriented. I have classes with white women and Herschel, and they are attracted to him. So it's not just Herschel Walker choosing white women. They want to go out with him."

Women, black or white, do tag along at Walker's side between classes. But Walker's roommate in McWhorter Hall, the athletes' dormitory, is Barry Young, a sophomore fullback, also a black youth from a small Georgia farm town; Walker's most frequent companion on campus, Daryll Jones, a sophomore cornerback, is a black youth from west Georgia, and Walker's favorite place on campus is his sister Veronica's room in Oglethorpe Dormitory, where Jones, Walker, and other black friends listen to music and talk.

There are few places other than Veronica's room for Walker to escape his star status. The phone in Walker and Young's small room rings constantly. "I take it off the hook when Herschel's not here," Young says. Walker has not a single memento on his side of the room, just his cowboy hat and a huge stereo tape deck [that is] rarely turned off. "I don't mind studying here. I can block it out. I can block it out sometimes even when I'm talking with somebody," Walker says.

Walker is maintaining a 3.2 grade point average on a 4-point system. This fall, Walker began classes at 7:50 AM with an hour-long physical-education course in karate (he is a brown belt); followed by a class in speech, propaganda, and communications; then American literature (Walker writes poems); and philosophy. He usually eats in the athletes' cafeteria at McWhorter, then spends an hour at the sports information department being interviewed by the press every Tuesday of the season. By 3:00 PM, he is on the practice field, exercising, running, hitting, and being hit.

For an hour every evening that he can, Walker drives downtown to the Athens Institute of Karate. "I love to go down there and kick on the bags," he says. "It's good for discipline. The philosophy of it is to help you keep control." He is trying to keep control on the football field as well: "This year, I have to prove I'm not a fluke. Then the year after I'm going to have to prove I've still got it. Then my senior year, I'll have to prove I haven't got the big head. It's like I'm always on trial and everyone is judging me."

The odds that Herschel Walker will remain physically capable of playing professional football decrease with every game he plays. He takes a pounding from men bigger than he is, but so far he has escaped serious injury. "You're a little sore after a game," Walker says, "but it's gone on Sunday. The whole team runs a mile about 9:00 Sunday morning, and that gets the soreness out." In return for this, Walker is getting a degree in criminology, the academic course that drew him to Georgia.

In a business sense, Herschel Walker plays football for the University of Georgia athletic department. The Bulldog football team earns nearly $5 million a year for the department. It costs the department less than $2 million to field the team. The profit comes from ticket sales and television revenue, from bowl appearances and souvenir sales, and it pays for every other intercollegiate sport Georgia plays, including $170,000 for the track team, which earns nothing but includes the Olympic sprinter Mel Lattany. By comparison, the Atlanta Falcons of the National Football League spent about $6 million on their team last year and made a profit, from television, of about the same. The potential profits from cable television are at the heart of a dispute between the NCAA and the College Football Association (CFA), composed of major power schools such as Georgia. The CFA wants to sign its own television contract, with its own rules for recruiting and rewarding the college talent seen on its shows.

There is a budget crunch throughout the nation on collegiate athletics. Dooley's department, for example, had to come up with an additional $250,000 last year to cover university tuition increases for students on athletic scholarships. This year, for the first time, the department has its national football title, an excellent team, Herschel Walker, and enormous publicity. And this year, the Bulldogs logo; the G on the helmets; UGA IV, the Bulldogs' mascot; and anything else that can be copyrighted has been. A promotion director was hired to market it all, including beer mugs, shirts, ceiling paddle fans in "limited edition," and other exotic items.

The week after Georgia's 44–0 thrashing of Tennessee, disk jockey Skinny Bobby Harper was broadcasting his morning show in Atlanta when a salesman from a small agency walked into the studio with a poster. "What a great poster of Herschel," Harper said. Herschel who? It is against NCAA rules to use the name of individual athletes to make money. There can be no Herschel Walker buttons on which the department gets its 6 percent royalty, the inaugural rate, and no Herschel Walker full-color wall posters.

So the poster in question has a black running back in Georgia uniform, the face in blurred motion, the No. 3 visible, but not the 4 of

Herschel Walker's famous 34—certain to be a retired number one day. Type on the poster only mentions Sir William Herschel, the 18th-century British astronomer, and how he discovered the planet Uranus. A group of Atlanta businessmen put that together, paying the 6 percent to the athletics department. On schemes such as this, the department hopes to be making $400,000 a year by the time Herschel Walker is a senior, if he stays that long.

Most hard-core football fans know Herschel Walker's favorite comedian is Richard Pryor. Asked who was portrayed in the poster, a department spokesman said, "Well, he's not skinny enough to be Richard Pryor."

Tony Barnhart, *What It Means to Be a Bulldog*

LINDSAY SCOTT:WIDE RECEIVER 1978-1981

In 2004 Tony Barnhart compiled a memoir from more than 70 Georgia Bulldogs, in their own words, for his book What It Means to Be A Bulldog. *Wide receiver Lindsay Scott, who caught the key 93-yard touchdown pass from Buck Belue to beat Florida during the 1980 championship season, looks back on that play and his experiences playing at Georgia from 1978 to 1981.*

It's funny, but when you're young you have no idea how a few seconds on a football field in Jacksonville, Florida, will change your life. You have to grow older and get a little perspective to realize the real impact of something like the touchdown play that beat Florida in 1980.

It's not something I talk about every day, but I don't mind if other people want to ask me about it. I'm flattered that they still remember because it was more than 20 years ago.

When I look back on my time at Georgia, I like to remember just hanging out with my teammates in the locker room. I like to remember getting ready for the games and the celebration after a game when we won. I like to remember the friendships that I made then that are so important to me today. For me, that was the real joy of my four years at Georgia. That's what being a Bulldog is all about.

When I was a senior at Wayne County High School in Jesup, Georgia, I was looking around outside the state. I wanted to go somewhere where I could get the opportunity to get the ball on a regular basis. My high school coach, John Donaldson, was a Georgia man, and I think he figured out that I would score a touchdown every four times I touched the ball. So he put together all kinds of ways for me to get the ball. That was the only drawback when I thought about Georgia, because they had a great history of running the ball—three yards and a cloud of dust, you know.

My dad really liked the Tennessee offense. Coach Johnny Majors had come to Tennessee, and they were known for sending a lot of great receivers to the NFL. But my mom really wanted me to go to Georgia because she wanted to come see me play. I had an older brother, Dennis, who went to Virginia Tech, and there was just no way that we could get up to Blacksburg to see him play very often.

The other thing was that I had developed a bond with Coach Mike Cavan. That made all the difference in the world. When Georgia signed Buck Belue at quarterback, I was convinced they would open up the offense because Buck was a great passer. So I decided to stay at home and go to Georgia.

I'll never forget my freshman year, in 1978. I expected to play early, and by the LSU game I was a starter. I was able to run the second-half kickoff back for a touchdown, and we went on to win that game, 24–17, over there in Baton Rouge. I wish I could explain what it felt like to do that in front of those 90,000 people. It was really something, and I believe that's when people started to notice what I could do. You always wonder as a young player if you can compete at this level. That's when I was sure that I could.

Later on that year we beat Georgia Tech, 29–28, in the wildest game I've ever been a part of. Buck came off the bench and brought us from behind to win that game. I know that was a big moment for him.

That was a good team for a lot of reasons, but the guy I looked up to was Willie McClendon, our running back. We played against a lot of good running backs, but nobody ran harder than Willie. I really looked to him for my inspiration.

I wish I knew what happened in 1979, when we went 6–5. We lost a lot of good players, like Willie, and that was a team that really needed to grow up. We were talented but still very young. That was such a weird year; we started by losing to Wake Forest, 22–21. We lost all of our nonconference games but kept winning the conference games until we got to Auburn, who beat us pretty good. But if we had beaten Auburn, we could have gone to the Sugar Bowl with a 6–5 record. That was really strange.

I'll never forget something that Coach Wayne McDuffie said during that time. Coach McDuffie once told us that we were happy winning on a regional level when we should be thinking on a national level. He believed that Georgia had everything it needed to compete for the national championship. Now, nothing was broken at Georgia, but he thought that we should be thinking bigger. I think our class listened to him. We thought we could do something big.

[Editor's note: In the spring of 1980, Lindsay Scott lost his football scholarship for one year after an altercation with an athletics department official, but was allowed to stay with the team and pay his own way to school. In late summer, he was involved in an automobile accident that left him with a concussion and several dislocated bones in his foot. One of the doctors told Scott's mother that he would never play football again.]

After the accident I did sit around for a while and wonder "why me?" But the honest answer was that I had never had to face any real adversity in my life. Things had always rocked along pretty well for me.

The fact is, I had to grow up a little bit. I'm sure that at some point every college kid goes through what I went through. It's just not all over the papers the next day. But that's part of being a college football player at a place like Georgia. I had forgotten who I was supposed to represent. I wasn't just representing myself. I was representing my family and my school. I had to learn that.

Yes, a doctor told my mother I would never play again, but that was a joke, because I knew I was coming back. I didn't care how hard I had to work. I know my mother was afraid for me, but she never questioned me when I said I was going back and that I was going to play. She never asked me not to play. She knew deep down inside that I was going to be all right.

It took a while before I felt right again. The foot healed up fine, but it took me a while to get my equilibrium completely back. I don't think I ever felt completely right until we got to Jacksonville to play Florida.

We weren't throwing the ball very much, but I understood why. Herschel Walker had come on as a freshman and had been an incredible running back. And with a player like that, you knew Coach Dooley was going to keep giving him the ball.

But you know how it is when you're a receiver—you want to catch the ball. It's funny now, but back then an article came out where a reporter asked some of us receivers if we wished we were throwing the ball more. Well, what would you expect us to say? Of course! What receiver doesn't want to catch the ball more?

But the article made it sound like we were unhappy with the way the offense was being run. Well, if you know Coach Dooley, you know that wasn't going to work. He pulled us aside the next day and politely told us what he thought. That was the last time we talked about that issue.

When we got to Jacksonville I had not caught a touchdown pass all season. We had played nine games, and I was shut out. We were winning, and I was happy about that, but catching a touchdown pass does wonders for your confidence. You feel like you're an important part of the offense.

And to be perfectly honest about it, I needed something good to happen to me. With everything that had gone wrong in my life—losing my scholarship and the accident—I just needed something to go my way for a change.

I really thought we were going to put Florida away. We jumped on top of them early, but all of a sudden they jumped ahead of us, 21–20. After all we had been through together, I just didn't see how we were going to let this thing slip away. And when they kicked the ball out of bounds at the 8-yard line things didn't look good.

I remember that in the huddle Nat Hudson wouldn't let anybody get down. We knew what we had to do. We had an All-American kicker in Rex Robinson. We just had to get it close enough to give Rex a shot.

The first two plays were really frustrating. Buck lost a yard scrambling on the first play, and on the second play they took me out of the game. I was thinking, "What the hell are you doing! You brought me here to make plays. We talked about it! And with the game on the line I'm on the sideline!" I just didn't understand.

But I was put back in the game on third down, and Coach George Haffner called left 76. All we wanted to do was get a first down and keep the drive alive.

My job was to go down and do a little curl pattern. I didn't know what was going on behind the line of scrimmage. All I knew was that Buck got me the ball, and when I caught it, I knew I had the first down.

But at that moment my mind went back to something that John Donaldson had taught me in high school. He always said, "Don't fall; keep on running after you catch the ball." So when I caught the ball and felt myself going down, I put my hand on the ground to steady myself and kept running. Once I caught my balance I saw a guy go down, and then I saw an opening.

When I started running, my first thought was that I could get us into field-goal range. After about 10 more yards it dawned on me, "Hell, I can take this thing to the house."

I have no idea who was behind me or how close they were, but I knew I was fast enough to outrun them if I just didn't fall down. And the second I got to the end zone it seemed like the whole world came down on top of me. Everybody called it a miracle. To me it was the greatest feeling in the world. It was the shot in the arm that I really needed.

Like I said before, I didn't understand the magnitude of that play for a long, long time. It began to sink in a little after we won the national championship. If we hadn't beaten Florida, 26–21, that day then we probably never would have gotten the chance to play Notre Dame in the Sugar Bowl.

That team was really special. We had that big play against Florida, but guys had been making big plays like that all year. Every week it was somebody different. I can't begin to tell you how many plays Scott Woerner made during the course of that season. It was incredible.

The fact that we're still talking about that play more than 20 years later tells me that it is something special. But it was just one great moment in the four years that I spent at Georgia—the best four years of my life.

At Georgia I had the opportunity to play ball, travel, and meet friends who would stick with me the rest of my life. I had a chance to be with a group of guys who could say that we were the best team in college football. Not a lot of people get to say that.

The entire Georgia experience affected the way I think about life. Sure, I've had to regroup a couple of times in my life. And when I did, I would go back to the lessons I learned at Georgia from Coach Dooley. When things get tough, you always go back and pull those lessons out of the closet. That's because they work.

For me, going to Georgia was a once-in-a-lifetime experience. There has never been anything else like it.

The New York Times

MAN IN THE RIGHT PLACE FOR GEORGIA

*Terry Hoage was a key playmaker for the Bulldogs from his "rover" posi-
tion in the defensive backfield in the early 1980s, leading the nation in
interceptions as a junior and receiving All-American honors twice. The
player Vince Dooley called "the greatest defensive player I ever coached"
talks about his playing philosophy in this piece from* The New York
Times, *which was published during his senior season.*

Standing by the nose of an F4-D Phantom jet in a photograph that
Vince Dooley is contemplating, Terry Hoage appears as intended.
"Like a fighter," said his coach. "A proper All-American, a proper can-
didate for the Heisman Trophy."

"I saw it as another tag for me to wear," said Hoage.

He looked much the same yesterday, not in uniform, but alert and
square-jawed, with hair cropped short in front and, fashionably, a bit
longer in back. After an appearance on the *Good Morning America*
show, before lunch at Sardi's, Hoage detailed the intricacies of playing
his position, defensive safety and rover on the Georgia football team.

"Everything is done on the run," he said, "to anticipate what will
happen. Everyone else works almost completely on assignment. But
my job is to react, consider everything scientifically in a matter of one
second and throw my body where it belongs as if I had no regard for
what happened to it."

Hoage was introduced about town yesterday with Steve Young, the
quarterback from Brigham Young, as representatives of the Kodak All-
America team, which is selected by college football coaches.

Dislikes "Cute Slogan"

When he was shown the photo of the jet and himself, now used as a
promotional poster for the Heisman, Hoage pushed it away. The
caption reads, "America's Top Two Defenders."

"Another cute slogan," said Hoage. "Really, I'm very removed from
the whole thing."

If Terry Hoage, a 21-year-old senior, is unaccustomed to celebrity status, it is understandable. He spent the first year of his college football career mostly not playing, until the week before the 1981 Sugar Bowl, when he blocked three field-goal attempts in practice. In the game against Notre Dame, he then blocked a field goal that set up the first score. Georgia went on to win.

He was an automatic starter as a sophomore. As a junior, he led the nation in interceptions, but the spotlight still was on Herschel Walker.

He was hardly recruited out of Huntsville High School in Texas. Georgia did not come to him; he solicited Georgia, and now he is acclaimed as the major reason that Georgia, without Walker, is still a major football power. The Bulldogs are not ranked first nationally, as they were last December in both news-agency polls, but they will go to the Cotton Bowl against Texas January 2 with a 9–1–1 record.

Walker decided games with breakaway runs. Hoage did it this past season with improbable interceptions and desperate field-goal blocks. Last year, in a full season, he made 101 tackles, and his 12 interceptions were the most in the country. This season, in eight games, before he sprained an ankle badly against Temple on October 29, he made 60 tackles and blocked three field-goal attempts.

"Please don't think that this is just the coach saying nice things," said Dooley, "but in all my years of coaching, I have never seen a defensive player who can consistently turn the most important play of the game, each game."

As the name of the position connotes, a rover's territory is the ground left uncovered. He is the last resort for a beaten defense, the one most likely to make the big play when it is called for. Hoage blocked two field goals in a game against Clemson to preserve a 16–16 tie. In the Bulldogs' 20–13 victory over Vanderbilt, he intercepted one pass in the end zone, and later, in the fourth quarter, he stretched his body out and diverted another one with the tip of his index finger. The intended receiver was wide open.

"I consider myself a hit man," Hoage said yesterday. "The idea is to run in such a way to cut down corners, either when sacking a quarterback or going for a kicker. But mainly, the thing is to accept the role of a defensive man. To find the pleasure in that.

"On offense, guys pull their socks all the way up. On defense, you're hanging on. You have to scrap around. It's more of a street fight than anything."

The struggle began in his senior year of high school when he was a starting quarterback and a strong safety. Hoage received several letters from the good football programs in the Southwest Conference. But then, suddenly, the schools drew back. It wasn't until later that Hoage and his parents discovered that a recruiter—either with Texas or Houston, they suspect—passed the word that he was too slow and "not a winner." Recruiters, thorough as they are, depend on hearsay and innuendo, and Hoage had become an untouchable.

If it weren't for a family friend at Sam Houston State University, where Hoage's father is a biology professor, Hoage would not have gone to Georgia. The friend had ties with Georgia of the Southeastern Conference, and at the family's request, he sent the school films of Hoage. Weeks later, Hoage was a Bulldog.

When Georgia plays Texas in the Cotton Bowl, his father says he will derive an added sense of satisfaction. "You go forward," said Terrell Hoage, "but honestly, I'd like to rub their noses in it."

His son is less bitter. Everything has worked out. Terry Hoage is looking forward to playing professional football. A genetics major, he has a 3.75 grade point average and is also considering applying to medical school one day. "I reject labels," he said. "That's why I can consider both.

"Off the field I'm individualistic. On the field I'm combative, but part of a team. On the field, my alter ego takes over to survive."

Alex Crevar, *Georgia* magazine

KICKING DOWN THE DOOR

In a poll taken in 2004, the Bulldogs' 26–23 victory over Clemson in 1984 was voted the best game ever played at Sanford Stadium. The hero of that game was Kevin Butler, who kicked an unforgettable 60-yard field goal for the winning points.

The Chicago Bears of the 1980s were so rough-and-tumble that they got rid of their cheerleaders because they didn't fit the team's image. The Monsters of the Midway had a defense that will forever rank as one of the NFL's most menacing, plus a 300-pound nose guard–turned-fullback known as "the Fridge" and a macho player-turned-coach named Ditka, whom his players affectionately called "Sybil."

The Bears also had a kicker from Stone Mountain, Georgia, who wore a helmet with one bar and rolled-up sleeves, exposing unkicker-like biceps even in the harshest Chicago winters. The tough-guy kicker was Kevin Butler, who made history at Georgia with a 60-yard field goal to beat Clemson. In December, Butler did it again when he was inducted into the College Football Hall of Fame—the only kicker ever to be so honored.

"Even the kicker had to be tough with the Bears," says the now-retired Butler, who was christened as a professional with a Super Bowl championship ring in his rookie season in 1985. "I made 11 kickoff tackles that first year; I worked out with the guys—and everyone loved it."

An all-state selection in soccer and as a defensive back and kicker on Redan High School's football team, Butler would likely have been a position player in college had he not suffered a knee injury in the first game of his senior year at Redan.

"I was upset that I couldn't be a position player," he recalls, "but it became a blessing, allowing me to concentrate on just being a kicker for the first time."

Following the injury, interest among recruiters waned. But Georgia head coach and athletics director Vince Dooley told Butler the Dogs still had a scholarship for him. It was the first of many times the future Hall of Fame coach would display confidence in the future Hall of Fame kicker.

It was one of those steamy September days in Athens when number-two ranked Clemson came to Stanford Stadium in 1984. The Tigers dominated the Bulldogs in the first half and Dooley's Dogs went to the locker room trailing 20-3. The Dogs battled back in the second half and with 11 seconds left and the game tied at 23, Georgia had the ball at the Clemson 43. Most teams would have opted for a desperation, Hail Mary fling into the end zone. But Dooley sent Butler out to try a 60-yard field goal—and never even bothered to ask if he had it in him.

"My longest practice kick was 78 yards," Butler recalls. "It wasn't so much a matter of distance as...just putting it through. Coach Dooley gave me the confidence I needed as a kicker."

"Heck, any time we got past the 50, Kevin would stand right in front of me on the sidelines," Dooley recalls. "He always wanted to kick the game-winner. What I remember most about that Clemson kick is that he could have made it from 70."

As soon as the ball left his foot, Butler knew he'd gotten enough of it. But he watched a second longer to make sure it held its line. It did, and all hell broke loose in Sanford Stadium.

"I ran to the student section," says Butler, "and then to the cheerleaders!"

"Yeah, and then you remembered I was no longer a cheerleader, and you came running to me on the sidelines!" says Butler's wife, the former Cathy Clement.

Butler's 60-yarder still ranks as the longest in Bulldogs history. He holds school records for most career field goals (77) and most points (353). He made 11 field goals beyond 50 yards and posted an NCAA record of 27 multiple-field-goal games.

Although Butler's kick to beat Clemson actually spurred some sportswriters to wonder if a kicker could compete for the Heisman Trophy, it wasn't his only highlight of that game. He kicked four field goals that day, including a 51-yarder. In his sophomore year in 1982, he kicked a game-winner against a Steve Young–led BYU team, a 59-yarder versus Ole Miss, and two field goals against Auburn to help Georgia clinch a third-straight SEC title. Butler's last kick as a Bulldog was a 72-yard attempt that came up a foot short of beating Florida State in the 1984 Citrus Bowl.

Butler helped Georgia compile a 38–8–2 record from 1981 to 1984, including two SEC titles, two Sugar Bowls, a Cotton Bowl, and the Citrus. He is a member of all-century teams selected by the Walter Camp Foundation, *Sports Illustrated,* and ABC Sports. He is the 13th Georgia player or coach inducted into the College Football Hall of

Fame and the sixth in the last eight years, including Terry Hoage and Herschel Walker.

"The difference between Kevin and any kicker I've coached was his competitive instinct," says Bill Hartman Jr., a Hall of Famer himself who coached UGA kickers from 1972 to 1995. "He was always a big part of any team—not just 'the kicker.'"

Asked whether he expects to be inducted into the Pro Football Hall of Fame, Butler shrugs.

"I don't get wrapped up in that stuff," he says. You do it because you love the sport. I would have traded all my NFL years for four more years of college. In college, it's for fun."

Selected as the Bears' fourth-round pick in the 1985 draft, Butler set 19 club records in 11 seasons; in 1989, he set a then-NFL record of 24 consecutive field goals without a miss.

Of his remarkable success in cold, blustery conditions, Butler says Soldier Field actually made him a *better* kicker.

"It's hard to kick in bad weather," he says. "To get better, I had to practice at Soldier Field as much as possible—no fun."

Butler finished his career with the Arizona Cardinals in 1997, retiring with 1,208 points, sixth most in NFL history among kickers. Q: What does he miss most? A: The paychecks. "When the time was right, we put football behind us and came home," says Cathy. "Georgia was always our goal."

Cathy and Kevin had business opportunities waiting for them. Cathy works at her mother's bridal shop, Formally Yours, in Lilburn. Kevin is vice president of Production Group International, which helps businesses achieve objectives through creative events. He actually began his business career even before his NFL career ended, joining forces with his late Bears teammate Walter Payton to develop golf courses and promote the NFL Pro Shop line of golf accessories.

"Being back in Georgia gives Cathy and me a chance to reconnect with the university," says Butler from his Sugarloaf Country Club home in Duluth, where he and Cathy live with their son and two daughters. "It's hard to be active with your alma mater when you're playing football during football season. But it's nice to be home because Athens is the place where we fell in love—and a place where we always feel loved."

Dave Kindred, *The Sporting News*

MORE THAN A PASSING GRADE

Dave Kindred visited with Eric Zeier in 1994, and the quarterback shared his thoughts on playing the position with the Sporting News *columnist.*

Five seconds to play in a big game and you are trailing 33–26. You are 12 yards from a touchdown that can beat a team much better than yours. A victory turns your season around. A coach signals in the play. He wants the smash game. The call is 272.

You have thrown the ball 64 times. Even Fran Tarkenton never did that at your school. You have completed 36 for 386 yards. You need 12 more yards.

Four receivers go wide, two on each side. The outside men run a hitch, straight downfield and turning to face you. The men inside run a flag, breaking toward the end-zone corners.

You like the play. But you have used the formation before. It can be no surprise. In the huddle, you say: "272." And you say: "Let's run it a new way."

We are talking quarterbacks with Eric Zeier, the Heisman Trophy candidate from the University of Georgia. He already belongs in Southeastern Conference lore with Archie Manning and Kenny Stabler, Joe Namath and Heath Shuler. Zeier, 21, is a career military man's son. He is a portrait of bubbling energy, eager to get at life's next play.

We are talking quarterbacks with a good one who is answering questions with bursts of words that leave the visitor's notebook a scribbly mess when all the visitor did was ask about putting together the perfect quarterback.

"Aikman's drop," Zeier says. "Marino's release. Montana's knowledge and feel. Elway's arm. Johnny Unitas's leadership."

Rat-a-tat-tat.

Zeier says he will name quarterbacks he has seen. But he went back 35 years for Unitas because he knew the stories.

"Unitas broke his nose in a game and kept on playing," Zeier says. "He just stopped it up with a bunch of mud. That's toughness and leadership. Getting up in pain, you're hurting, and you say, 'Let's do it.' You're hurt, but you don't stay down. You get up and lead your team to victory."

Before his 65th pass against Florida, Zeier read the coach's signal for smash, 272, and then told the inside receiver on the left side: "Let's change routes. No flag. Make it a post."

Zeier hoped Florida's defender would be late to cover, even a heartbeat late. Zeier would turn his eyes to the outside. A "hard look," he called it, hoping to persuade the defender the ball might be thrown out there, a heartbeat's indecision. "Then we've got him beat," Zeier says.

The ball left Zeier's hands...and he says he thought he heard a whistle.

Some folks in Georgia get buried wearing red and black, the university's colors. College football means a lot to a lot of people. Older than basketball, in more places than big league baseball, it fills stadiums with more people than live in any but some states' largest two or three cities.

Sanford Stadium holds 86,117 Georgia worshipers, many of whom fall to all fours and woof in the manner of UGA, the bulldog mascot. Such behavior was perfected during Vince Dooley's 25 seasons, particularly in 1980 when the team won a national championship on Herschel Walker's running.

Dooley's successor, Ray Goff, recruited Zeier out of suburban Atlanta's Marietta High School (chosen by the Zeiers for the quarterback's last two high school seasons—the first two were in Heidelberg, Germany).

In his sixth season, Goff needs to be good after last season's 5–6 record. And for Georgia to be good, it needs Zeier to be great.

We know he can throw. We know he is Joe Montana's size, 6'2", 205 pounds. But we also know Montana works with instincts and quickness that make possible the unlikely. Whether or not Zeier has such gifts, we will soon find out.

Last winter, wondering about the pros, Zeier canvassed 14 NFL teams and decided he was a third-round draft choice at best. So he returned to Georgia for his senior season. *The Atlanta Journal-Constitution* reports that NFL scouts now rate Zeier as the country's number-one quarterback prospect.

"His throwing motion is pure beauty," says Dexter Wood, his high school coach. Florida coach Steve Spurrier, himself once a quarterback who won the Heisman, says Zeier throws "a nice, catchable ball." Bill Curry of Kentucky on how seldom Zeier is intercepted: "That's the kind of stuff Bart Starr and Johnny Unitas used to do."

A whistle? When? No one stopped playing. The defender held his ground for an instant, just as Zeier hoped. He had him beat. The quarterback didn't even look at receiver Jerry Jerman. He knew where he would be. A perfect pass. Touchdown.

Only there had been a whistle. Georgia's outside receiver on the left side, Anthone Lott, had called timeout an instant before the snap. No play. Some teams find ways to lose.

"I heard the whistle right before I threw," Zeier says. "I didn't do any celebrating."

Still five seconds to play. Another pass. Interference. One more play, no time on the clock. Zeier's 65th pass. Incomplete. "Their linebacker made a good play," Zeier says. "I had nowhere to throw it where it could be caught."

We are talking quarterbacks with the only passer in SEC history to throw for 500 yards in a game. He is also the only SEC player to throw for more than 400 yards more than once, doing it three times last season. What he does better than most is see theory on film and take it to the field where he makes it real for his team. Only quarterbacks get to do that.

So a visitor asks Zeier one more question. Would he like any other position as much? Zeier tries to say yes; he is a football player, and he would play anywhere. "But," he says, eager to make a play on this day of Montana and Unitas and Aikman, "I love being a quarterback."

Marc Lancaster, *Athens Banner-Herald*

BAILEY'S CHAMPS CHEER DRAFT

Each year most of the top college draft prospects attend the nationally televised NFL draft extravaganza in New York City. Not Champ Bailey, who in 1999, when he was made the top pick of the Washington Redskins, elected to share his big day with his family and friends at home in Georgia.

Kicking off ESPN's 10-hour coverage of the 1999 National Football League draft on Saturday, announcer Chris Berman bragged on the exhaustive coverage his network would provide. With cameras in 27 of the 31 NFL cities, he surmised, "If you have a Rand McNally atlas, we've got you covered."

But for the 2,245 residents of this southeast Georgia hamlet on the fringes of the Okefenokee Swamp, the fact that Berman and his crew were nowhere near here Saturday is what made it so special. This was Georgia cornerback Champ Bailey's day, and he couldn't have lived it anywhere but here, with anyone but his people.

So Bailey didn't follow the lead of the nation's other top-rated players, like Kentucky's Tim Couch, Oregon's Akili Smith, and Texas's Ricky Williams, by going to New York City for the NFL's official draft party. On a day defined by decisions, this one was easy for Bailey.

"When they told me I had a choice, I was like, 'I'm going home,'" Bailey said Saturday. "I knew they would do something real nice for me, and it doesn't get much better than this."

This was nothing less than Bailey, at age 20, rejoicing in a *This is Your Life*–type moment at home surrounded by those he has known since childhood. Here, in what some would consider a run-down lot in a not-so-pretty neighborhood just off Long Street, Bailey heard the words that will make him the richest man in town (he's already the most famous): "With the seventh pick in the 1999 NFL draft, the Washington Redskins select Champ Bailey, cornerback from Georgia."

That announcement by NFL commissioner Paul Tagliabue on national television ignited a roar from the crowd of a few hundred that had gathered to fête Bailey on the biggest day of his life.

Black and white, young and old gathered in a lot that had previously held two vacant, dilapidated houses. Saturday, new wood chips coated the tree-lined lot, with a humble stage (built on the foundation of one of the razed residences) to one side and a huge tent to the other. A pair of cable-wired televisions hung from poles so all could watch the proceedings as the scent of fried fish, barbecued ribs, and seasoned chicken drifted by.

This was not Madison Square Garden, and nobody wore a suit. But how could the Bailey family throw any other kind of party but this?

"Obviously, the NFL and ESPN would rather Champ had been in New York, to parade him out, and he chose to be in his hometown with his family and his friends," said UGA assistant athletic director Freddy Jones, himself a Folkston native. "To me, that shows you how much the community means to Champ and how much Champ means to the community. It's a big day. But this is why Champ is the player he is, because he's never forgotten his roots, and the whole family's been that way."

Indeed, everywhere one turned Saturday, there was a Bailey. From Champ to younger brother Boss, to mother Elaine, to father Roland Sr., to an endless array of cousins, aunts, and uncles. The only missing piece was older brother Ronald, who had a big day of his own Saturday, making his NFL Europe debut as a cornerback with the Frankfurt Galaxy.

Even though Champ said he was disappointed that his brother and former Georgia teammate couldn't be here for the party, there were enough hugs and high fives to make up for Ronald's absence.

"It's a big accomplishment, somebody finally doing something positive," said 23-year-old Sylvester Bailey, Champ's first cousin. "It reflects on the whole community. It's nice to see somebody finally make it, and it just happens to be my cousin. I'm proud of him."

Sylvester wasn't alone. As Champ fielded call after call on his grandmother's cordless phone and two cellular phones wielded by his agent, Jack Reale, kids would timidly approach their hero and ask for an autograph, which he happily provided. Adults would appear quickly to shake his hand or clap him on the shoulder like long-lost relatives in a close-knit family—which, in this town, they really are.

Somehow, the celebration of Charlton County's favorite son turned into an affirmation for the entire community, which like the Bailey family is not particularly rich or glamorous—a fact punctuated by the roosters happily wandering down Long Street, oblivious of the party. Things are not always easy in a town like this, as Sylvester Bailey alluded to. There is unemployment, and there are those who struggle with drugs and alcohol.

But Saturday, there was simply happiness, and everyone shared in it.

"I think in any community, when one of your own does well—and this is really considered doing well—you've got to be real excited and real pleased," said Charlton County High School football coach Rich McWhorter, who was lucky enough to coach all of the Bailey brothers and several other players who went on to major colleges. "Any time a positive happens in these days and times, you've really got to celebrate it."

How giddy was everyone here Saturday afternoon? Even Gators were welcome.

University of Florida wide receiver Travis Taylor, a childhood friend and opponent of Bailey's, hobnobbed with Georgia players Tony Gilbert, Quentin Davis, and Terin Smith at the party, proving that this day transcended just about any kind of rivalry.

"It's great to see Champ going seventh overall in the draft," said Taylor, who played against Bailey's Charlton County teams as a standout at Camden County High School in nearby Kingsland. "It's just great to see somebody you know and played against and played with doing good things."

Perhaps that's what drew everyone here in the first place—the famous Bailey family humility. Among those at the party, it was hard to find someone that didn't want to see Bailey succeed.

"He deserves everything he gets," said Gilbert, a freshman linebacker at UGA. "I hope God blesses him and he has a good career in the pros."

Not that anyone expects Bailey to fail—he never has, going back to when he first played football as an eight-year-old. "I always thought he would [make the NFL], even in high school," said Sylvester Bailey. "Man, I knew that ever since he was playing for the Folkston Falcons in Pop Warner. When he was little—I'm a couple of years older—and me and his brother Ronald, we always used to play and make him and Boss play against us. He was making us look bad then. Track, football, basketball—it didn't matter."

It still doesn't for the man Georgia coach Jim Donnan calls the best athlete he's ever been around. Champ Bailey has always been dominant in any sport he tried, and he's never sought any other goal than the one he achieved Saturday.

"That's a football player's dream, to make it to this level, and if you don't think you can do it then [as a kid], you probably won't do it," said Champ. "It's just like I tell these kids now today that I see, they can make it. I see a lot of potential. Even if they're not playing now, starting tomorrow or next year even, they can do it."

It was an unusually strong statement for the normally soft-spoken All-American. His eyes even got a bit watery as he delivered those lines. But it was just one of those days, one few people here will ever forget.

Just after 2:00 PM Saturday, the line for home-cooked food grew longer as Bailey continued to field calls from well-wishers. At the back corner of the stage, the disc jockey turned on his sound system and pumped out the first strains of music to keep the party rolling into the evening hours.

The first song?

"We Are Family," by Sister Sledge.

Nothing else would do on this day.

Lee Shearer, *Athens Banner-Herald*

D. J. SHOCKLEY: QUARTERBACK EARNS RESPECT

D. J. Shockley proved that good things come to those who wait. His patience and perseverance after sitting behind David Greene for four years paid off in 2005 as he blossomed into a star and had one of the best statistical seasons ever among Georgia quarterbacks.

D. J. Shockley won't go down in University of Georgia football history as one of the all-time statistical leaders at quarterback, but he'll surely be remembered as one of the most respected.

"He's a great young man," said Georgia offensive coordinator Neil Callaway.

"He does have a lot of high character," said former UGA sports information director and tennis coach Dan Magill, who's seen them all since the 1930s. "He's an outstanding person."

Entering the 2005 season, Georgia football fans knew Shockley would make news, since he was the Bulldogs' new starting quarterback, but were not sure what kind, since he'd spent the first four years of his career as a redshirt and bench-warming backup.

The story line on Shockley is this: as new coach Mark Richt's first signee, Shockley comes to UGA in 2001 as one of the nation's top quarterback prospects, only to find himself in the shadow of David Greene, who starts for four years, becoming the winningest quarterback in NCAA Division I-A history. Shockley becomes friends with Greene and never complains, though he admits it's frustrating to wait, especially after it becomes clear to Shockley in 2002 that he's not going to be the starting quarterback at Georgia for the next two years. He considers transferring to another school but doesn't, even though his coaches say Shockley could have been a two- or three-year starter at many other big-time football schools.

Instead, Shockley sticks, being a cheerleader and a student carrying a clipboard on the sideline.

"He waited patiently, cheering his teammates on, never saying 'I ought to play more' or anything like that," according to Magill. "It makes him admired greatly by everyone who knows him."

Finally, Greene graduates and Shockley's turn comes at last. In his final year of eligibility, he becomes the starter, getting one year to show the world what he can do in what is surely one of the world's most high-pressure jobs, quarterback for the Georgia Bulldogs.

More than a few of the hundreds of thousands of fans who follow the Bulldogs were nervous about Shockley.

There weren't many doubters at the end of the season, though.

"He came through with flying colors," Magill said.

Shockley threw 21 touchdown passes, a season total surpassed by just two other UGA quarterbacks, the celebrated Greene, Georgia's all-time passing leader, and Eric Zeier, who holds the single-season record with 24 touchdown passes.

Shockley ended the season first among Southeastern Conference quarterbacks in passing efficiency.

"We knew he was a good runner, but we didn't know how great a passer he was," Magill said.

Shockley came into the season dogged by what he said was his greatest weakness, trying to do too much. Trying to pass into the end zone, for example, even when no receivers were open—a sure formula for an interception.

By the second game, he had that one beaten.

"I realized I don't have to make every play on every series," he said.

Only one player in the 114-year history of Georgia football had a higher "touchdown responsibility" (touchdown passes plus those he scored himself) than Shockley's 25 this year—the legendary Frank Sinkwich, who had 27 in 1942, the year Sinkwich became UGA's first Heisman Trophy winner.

Most important, in the merciless eyes of the hundreds of thousands of Bulldogs faithful, in Shockley's one season as a starter he led Georgia to a 10–2 record and the SEC championship, something his celebrated predecessor at quarterback, Greene, managed just once in four years. This year's SEC championship is Georgia's second in four years, but it also was only the university's second in 22 years.

"He's had a very good year. We're all extremely happy for him," Callaway said.

And it wasn't just because he can chuck a football more than 80 yards. In Richt's system, the quarterback doesn't just throw and hand off the ball. It's also his duty to read defenses at the line of scrimmage and change the play if necessary, something Shockley did about once each offensive series this season, the quarterback estimated in a recent interview.

Shockley's years of patient waiting, followed by this year of quietly and confidently making the best of his chances, seemed to lift the whole team this season, Callaway said.

"I think it's rubbed off on our whole football team," Callaway said. "I think it shows extremely strong character."

But his athletic accomplishments and leadership are just part of why the old guard like Magill thinks so highly of the 22-year-old North Clayton High School alum, who graduated with honors at this month's UGA fall semester commencement.

Robert Miles, director of a life skills program for UGA athletes, remembers a day last summer when Shockley was helping to shepherd a group of children, some with mental disabilities, around UGA's football practice field. One little girl decided she didn't want to move when it was time to go, causing a bit of consternation for both the UGA people and staffers from the children's summer camp.

But D.J., a name young Donald Eugene took for himself when he got tired of being called "Donald Duck" by his teasing grammar-school classmates, knew just what to do, Miles said. He calmly asked the little girl if she'd like to go for a ride in a golf cart, swung her up in it, then drove off with her.

Shockley puts in serious volunteer hours and always will agree, time permitting, to make public appearances when children are involved, and especially children with disabilities, Miles said. What impresses Miles about Shockley is a genuine humility, he said.

"It just warms my heart to help out with them," Shockley says. "I think you have to focus on kids because they're the up-and-coming generation."

Shockley's two younger brothers have profoundly shaped the way he looks at children, at people with disabilities, and at his own life. His brothers, Xavier and Nicholas, suffer from a condition called fragile X syndrome, which left them with learning disabilities. Seeing them struggle with things that Shockley finds so easy has made the young athlete look at life differently, he said.

"It really made me not take for granted the little things you can do, like tying your shoes or driving your car," he said.

He's learned a lot from his brothers, Shockley said, but also from his parents, Don and Tanya Shockley.

And his father, a high school football coach, especially taught him that as a star quarterback, he can't avoid being a role model, good or bad—and that even one small black eye, made public, can outweigh a lot of good things.

Just part of the job description, he knows.

Mark Richt, shown here celebrating a win over Tennessee in 2005, has brought Georgia's football program back to a national stature it hadn't experienced since the Dooley era.

Section III
THE COACHES

John F. Stegeman, *The Ghosts of Herty Field*

POP WARNER
OF GEORGIA

The immortal Pop Warner's role in the early history of Georgia football is detailed in the following chapter from The Ghosts of Herty Field *by John F. Stegeman. The editor and publisher are grateful to his wife, Janet Allais Stegeman, for permission to reprint this chapter here.*

In a remote section of the 1895 *Pandora*, the University of Georgia annual, appears this sentence: "The management has secured a trainer in the person of Glenn S. Warner. ..." Thus was announcement made of the start of one of the great coaching careers in the history of American football.

"Pop" Warner had just finished his playing days at Cornell, where he had captained his team, and had signed a 10-week contract to coach the 1895 Georgia 11 for a salary of $34 per week. He arrived in Athens on September 15 and, after walking to the athletic field, beheld a sight he would never forget. There was no fence around the field, practically no grass on the playing area, and "quite a few rocks were sticking out of the bare surfaces." And on the field to greet him were only a dozen players from which to build a team. Remembering his own playing days at Cornell, where football was a thriving, glamorous sport, Warner suddenly felt quite homesick.

But it didn't take long for prospects to brighten. When more boys came out for the team, Coach Warner was able to put together a substantial line and a fleet backfield. Quarterback Craig Barrow was "cool, quick, and a fine sprinter"; Captain Herb Stubbs was a strong punter and superb tackler; "Cow" Nalley, former star center now transferred to the backfield, was hard to bring down; and Ed Pomeroy was a good man in the clutch. The only trouble with Fred Morris, also a backfield candidate, was that he was so fast he consistently outran his interference.

Coach Warner's first victory came when Georgia romped over Wofford in the opener at Athens, 34–0. This set the stage for the clash with North Carolina, Georgia's most illustrious foe up until that time. The Tar Heels had been playing football seven years to Georgia's three, and their annual game with Virginia was well on the way to becoming a southern classic. It was a feather in Georgia's cap just to have Carolina on the schedule, even if the Red and Black was considered outmatched.

The game was played at Atlanta's Athletic Park, and some of the spectators, unwilling to remain on the sidelines, stationed themselves on the field squarely in back of the offensive team. One of these was John Heisman, the Auburn coach, who was scouting Georgia. Early in the game, North Carolina, backed up near its own goal line, sent its punter, [George] Stephens, back in kick formation. Rushed too badly to get his punt away, Stephens retreated a few yards only to find himself trapped between the oncharging Georgia linemen and the fans who had lined up behind the Carolina team. Coach Heisman, for one, had to duck to keep out of the way. Finally, in desperation, Stephens flung the ball forward, over the scrimmage line, into the arms of a startled team-mate, [Joel] Whitaker, while Georgia's secondary watched in disbelief. "Before the crowd was aware of it," wrote a reporter, "Whitaker was running through all obstructions like lightning with the ball, and had touched the ground back of the Georgia goal."

Since the forward pass had no place in the rules of the day, the fans were in an uproar. But the referee allowed the play to stand, with the observation that he "didn't see it." Men began squaring off, and "only the presence of Chief Connolly and the quick and determined work of the patrolmen prevented a general fight." Order was restored, and the game went on to its conclusion without another score being put on the board.

The Stephens -to-Whitaker pass became something of a cause célèbre. "It was clearly a fluke," said the *Constitution*, while the *Journal* called it a "clever trick." The play went down in athletic history as the first of its kind in the annals of football; it later would have an impor-tant role in the development of the modern sport. Ten years after the game, John Heisman wrote to Walter Camp of the incident, recom-mending that such a play be legalized in order to open up the game. The following year, 1906, the forward pass officially entered the rule book.

North Carolina evidently felt some guilt over the spectacular play and, immediately upon its return to Chapel Hill, accepted Georgia's challenge to come back and play the game over again five days later. The rematch was set for the same field on October 31, which was to be Atlanta Day at the huge World's Fair being held at Piedmont Park. Although Athletic Park was several miles removed from the exposition, it was anticipated that a large segment of the fair crowd would be lured to the gridiron.

But things did not work out as well as had been expected. Atlanta Day happened to fall on the same date that an earthquake was felt throughout the United States, Atlanta included. "A great many people were awakened at an unusual and unreasonable hour this morning," said the *Journal*, "and a great many were also badly scared." Football was crowded out of the general conversation that morning, but by noon a few diehards had inquired of the weather bureau what conditions they might expect by game time. "I don't know," said a weatherman. "Earthquakes are not in my line."

As it turned out, a miserably cold rain began to fall, and only 350 spectators showed up at Athletic Park. By the end of the game, "the players looked more like well-diggers than anything else." Still, the teams put on a remarkably good show, with Carolina winning once again, 10–6. This time the Georgians went home satisfied they were beaten.

The team ran into foul weather again on November 9, but beat Alabama at Wildwood Park in Columbus, 30–6. It was the first intercollegiate game in the south Georgia city, but the crowd, because of "the drenching rain together with the inequality of the teams, lost all interest…before it was over."

Nine days later Georgia was back in Atlanta for a Monday game with Sewanee. Early in the first half, Georgia's "Cow" Nalley blocked a punt with Sewanee recovering on the scrimmage line. "The Georgia boys claimed the ball," wrote a *Constitution* reporter, "and Referee Dorsey was appealed to. He pleaded ignorance of the rules." (It seems that Mr. Dorsey had been sitting in the stands ready to enjoy the game when he was asked to serve as referee. He informed the captains he was "somewhat rusty" but got the job anyway.) The matter of the blocked kick was referred by Dorsey to the umpire, a Mr. Seixas, who, after chasing Coach Warner off the field, decided in Georgia's favor. A touchdown followed quickly, and tempers began to flare.

A short time later, Georgia tackle W. B. Kent, who once was criticized by a reporter for being "too polite," came into conflict with Whitaker, a Sewanee end. "Kent was slugged by Whitaker," said the *Constitution*, "and a lengthy squabble ensued. Umpire Seixas ordered Whitaker out of the game but very wrongly said he would let him come back if Captain Stubbs would consent. … After much unnecessary kicking…Whitaker attempted to show a spot on his leg where he claimed Kent had bitten him. There was no bruise, however. Captain [Stnley] Blalock [of Sewanee] declared he would not play if Whitaker went out, but finally the matter was adjusted, Whitaker leaving the game." Georgia went on to win, 22–0.

On November 24, under a headline, "Looks Like Robbery," a *Constitution* reporter told the story of Georgia's defeat by Vanderbilt in Nashville on the day before. Midway in the second half, with the score 0–0, Georgia's Pomeroy, after a handoff from Barrow, was piled up in the middle of the line. Pomeroy yelled, "Down," an act that normally ended a play in that day regardless of the referee's whistle. But seconds later, Elliott of Vanderbilt was seen holding the ball aloft. Georgia claimed he had merely picked it up after the scrimmage and was handing it to Walter Cothran, the Red and Black center, prior to the next play. At any rate, said the report, "Someone cried run, and Elliott ran, making a touchdown."

A furious Pop Warner rushed out on the field to register his complaint, but again he met his match. W. L. Granberry, the referee, informed the Georgia coach that he was a Princeton graduate, class of 1885, that he had officiated at every game in Nashville since that time, and that, moreover, he had never had a previous complaint. This was too much for Warner. He gathered his Georgia boys around him and walked off the field. Vanderbilt was awarded the victory, 6–0.

The final game, against Auburn, was scheduled for noon of Thanksgiving Day as an added attraction of the World's Fair at Piedmont Park. The playing field was laid out on the eastern border of the exposition grounds, which had been graded for Buffalo Bill's Wild West Show. The early kickoff was planned to allow the spectators to see the game and still have time to enjoy John Philip Sousa's band and attend the exhibits later in the day.

Actually the game started at 3:00 after a long argument over the officials. Both teams agreed on the referee, linesman, and timekeeper, but could not come to terms regarding the umpire. The Georgians wanted Mr. Seixas, who had satisfied them with his work previously, while Auburn preferred a Mr. Taylor for a similar reason. In a last-ditch compromise, both men were appointed and the game was on.

By that time, things were in a chaotic state. A good number of the 60,000 visitors to the fair that day crowded onto the playing field area, many of them curiosity seekers who had never before seen a football game. The condition of the playing field, which had been romped over for weeks by Buffalo Bill's cowboys, Indians, and horses, can well be imagined. "The beginning of the game was the scene of the wildest and most disgraceful confusion," wrote a reporter. "The spectators massed about the players and only a select and energetic few could see the game at all." Finally a student, "with white cap and glasses," relieved the situation temporarily by tearing down a wire from the grandstand and improvising a fence on the sideline.

The Georgians were favored because of their powerful showing against North Carolina, Sewanee, and Vanderbilt. But they had neglected to scout Auburn, while the Alabamians' new coach, John Heisman, had personally watched his opponents perform. Georgia learned its lesson quickly. Reynolds Tichenor, the flea-sized Auburn quarterback, seized control of the game and exploited Georgia's weaknesses, sending his running backs on repeated long gains.

Georgia found itself behind, 10–0, before finally getting a second-half drive underway. The *Constitution* described the scene: "Ball is on Auburn's 10-yard line. Excitement is intense. The crowd has poured upon the field and is absolutely unmanageable. Nalley goes one yard, Farrell five. The men can hardly hear the signals. Kent, with goal three yards away, springs around left end, making a detour of 20 yards and getting a touchdown."

But that was Georgia's last assault. Auburn charged back upfield, through the Georgia line and milling crowd, and made the clinching score. Georgia was upset, 16–6.

Pop Warner's first team had not been a success in the won-lost column, but the people were not deceived. "His excellent work has been seen constantly," wrote an Athens correspondent. "He has built up the team wonderfully in the short time he has been with us." Warner was asked to coach the 1896 team with a $6-a-week raise in salary, which, under a 12-week contract, gave him a total income of $480. "I will always prize that contract," Warner said. "My first raise! ... The Georgia management [told me] they wanted to beat Auburn if they lost every other game."

Harry Hodgson, Athens correspondent of the *Constitution*, wrote of the Georgia football spirit on October 11, 1896: "Nearly 2,000 Athenians regularly line the bleachers and watch with great interest the tumbling, running, wrestling contests of the players as they work to get themselves in shape for the big games that are to come this season. Athens has football fever. Athenians...are all enthusiastic about the great modern game. The football vocabulary is used in every household—the punts, rushes, crisscrosses, and scrimmage of the players are discussed around every fireplace. ... Every member of the family has an opinion about the merits of the football men and the chances of the university 11 defeating the teams of rival colleges in the games this fall."

Hodgson had visited Yale and compared the practices of the great New England team with those of Georgia: "The first contrast between the two teams was striking. The candidates for Yale's team came running upon the field from their dressing room in a body. The candidates for the Georgia team came one by one...and in pairs. Some arrived an hour before the others. They walked on the field leisurely, some singing. Others were lacing up their canvas jackets as they came and presented unmistakable signs of laziness. Finally about 25 candidates were on the Athens gridiron. Not one has done more than kick the ball, and more than an hour has been wasted. The Georgia men brought out two footballs for the entire crowd. ... The Yale crowd had one pigskin for every three men on the field."

The correspondent described some of the prospects: "Arthur Clark is a popular Atlanta back whose great disadvantage is his lack of weight. He is full of fire and speed. ... He is a hero to all of the small boys in

Athens. ... ["Von"] Gammon is a promising youth. He is but 16 years old and a freshman, but he punts like a veteran. He lacks confidence in himself and does not have much experience. ... [Hatton] Lovejoy has the right kind of grit."

Georgia beat Wofford, 26–0, in the opener, and on the last day of September met North Carolina at Brisbine Park in south Atlanta, the football team's first visit to the field that would be the scene of many a later triumph and heartbreak. There was one glaring defect in the area, a perceptible slope downward from the north goal to the south, forcing the team defending the latter goal to work its way uphill.

Early in the game the Tar Heels, although moving downhill, failed on a last-down gamble deep in their own territory, and Georgia got a quick 6–0 lead on Fred Price's touchdown and Hatton Lovejoy's conversion. Carolina rallied immediately. "[Fabius] Heyward came dashing through," read the report, "and dodged Lovejoy beautifully, placing the ball right between Georgia's goal posts. [Arthur] Belden kicked an easy goal to tie the score."

Minutes later Belden "made a beautiful punt," the ball going over the Georgia fullback's head. (*Safety-man* was not yet a football term.) "Lovejoy, a crack outfielder, tried to make a baseball play out of it. Speeding back and leaping into the air, he reached over his shoulder for the ball. It hit his fingers and rolled over the goal," where Carolina recovered for a touchdown.

The lineups:

Georgia	Position	North Carolina
Wight	LE	White
Price	LT	Wright (Capt.)
Blanche	LG	Neville
Atkinson	C	Joyner
Middlebrooks	RG	Carson
Kent	RT	Seagle
Watson	RE	Best
Gammon	QB	Green
Nalley (Capt.)	LH	Heyward
Cothran	RH	Moore
Lovejoy	FB	Belden

Coach Warner, who always cruised up and down the sidelines to keep abreast of the play, "was on the spot of the tragedy," Lovejoy recalled. "Pop shook his finger at me and shouted, 'Well, you have certainly played hell.'" Thereafter Warner ordered Lovejoy, the fullback, and Gammon, the quarterback, to trade places on defense, ending an old football precedent and setting a new one. Until that time fullbacks had invariably played in the hindmost position in the secondary.

Georgia tied the game again, 12–12, when Wright Blanche, dropping back of the line from his guard position, ran for a 30-yard touchdown. Just before the half ended, Blanche scored again, Lovejoy kicked goal, and Georgia took a surprise 18–12 lead at intermission.

It was nearly dark when the second half began, but plenty of football was played in the eight minutes of daylight left. Gammon punted out of bounds at the Carolina 5, and when Belden went back of his goal to kick for the Tar Heels, Blanche and Billy Kent broke through to block it. "When the referee made the men pile off," said the report, "both these Georgians were found hugging the ball" behind the goal line. Lovejoy again converted.

Carolina tried to get back in the game before nightfall, and Heyward crossed the Georgia goal. But when Belden missed the kick, Carolina still trailed, 16–24, and made no complaint when the officials called the game. A great southern upset had been scored.

Georgia returned to its own field to beat Sewanee, 26–0, on November 9. Then with only one more game on its schedule, the team spent the rest of the month preparing for the Thanksgiving clash with Auburn.

Pop Warner versus John Heisman! These are great names in football lore today, but in 1896 they were scarcely known a mile away from the Georgia and Auburn campuses. Both men were in the early years of their coaching careers; both had undefeated, untied teams. There was no conference championship to be played for, but the supremacy of a large segment of the Southland was on the line. Between the two teams, they had conquered all opposition in five different states.

More than 8,000 spectators, advertised as the largest crowd ever to see a game south of Philadelphia, crowded Brisbine Park. "Small boys…began to climb up on the roofs of the houses around the grounds," wrote a *Constitution* reporter. "Soon they lined every point of vantage that allowed the slightest view of the grounds. They looked like black birds squatted on top of the houses and perched up on the limbs of trees."

The lineups:

Georgia	Position	Auburn
Wight	LE	Mixen
Walden	LT	Harvey
Walker	LG	Nelson
Atkinson	C	Milkar
Blanche	RG	Sargeant
Kent	RT	Pierce
Daugherty	RE	Byrum
Gammon	QB	Tichenor
Nalley	LH	Williams

Georgia	Position	Auburn
Cothran	RH	Purifoy
Lovejoy	FB	Stokes

Captain Nalley, a five-year veteran who had played on every Georgia team, won the toss. The wind was sweeping up the field northward, so he decided to defend the south, or downhill, goal. Auburn kicked off, and the game that followed, by all accounts, was the best the Deep South had ever seen.

It began as a defensive struggle. "Von Gammon, the star quarterback of the Athens team, was given many opportunities to kick, and right royally did he do it," said the report. "With that good right of his, time and again he drove the pigskin into the air...toward Auburn's goal. One of his kicks sped 50 yards over the heads of the Auburnites."

After one of Gammon's kicks, Auburn fumbled in its own territory and Kent recovered for Georgia. Up to now, said a reporter, "[Auburn] appeared to have caught on to Georgia's signals. Every time Captain Nalley gave a signal, Captain Tichenor would call out to his men the trick the Georgians were about to play." It was at this point that Georgia dropped behind the line of scrimmage while Nalley gave a signal out of earshot of the Auburn team. This act later got wide credit as being football's first huddle but, according to the players themselves, was just an impromptu gathering to discuss the "trick" that followed.

"Captain Nalley...ordered a series of plays [four at a time]," wrote the *Constitution* reporter. "[They] are run off as fast as the men can line up, without any signals whatever. Every man knew just what play was to be put in practice. Without a word they hammered into [the] line, skirted the ends, bucked between guard and tackle, and carried the ball eight and 10 yards at a time toward Auburn's goal. Without a loss they plunged headlong into their opponents and carried the oval clean across Auburn's goal line." Lovejoy went the last foot and then kicked the goal, giving Georgia a 6–0 halftime lead.

To start the second half came another Warner trick. Georgia previously had kicked off deep into enemy territory at every opportunity, and Auburn now lined up its entire team near its own goal line. The Alabamians anticipated forming a flying wedge for their receiver, but Gammon, of Georgia, merely nudged the kickoff 15 yards downfield, where Nalley claimed the ball for Georgia. The onside play surprised and unnerved Auburn, and Georgia soon had another touchdown. Walter Cothran scored on an eight-yard run with Gammon flattening the last Auburn defender. Lovejoy again converted.

Auburn came back to score the hard way, on the higher end of the field. ("It was an uphill battle," Coach Heisman quipped.) Then, with

Georgia leading by only 12–6, the Alabamians threatened to tie the score on the brilliant punt returns of Reynolds Tichenor. The Auburn star recalled how he once almost met disaster. He was sprawled on the ground when a big Georgia lineman jumped at him, knees first, but Tichenor rolled out of the way just in time. "That fellow was very polite," the Auburn quarterback said. "We both got up and he apologized very profusely for having missed me."

The game finally ended, and Georgia's first perfect season was over. Few of the heroes were still around when the next all-winning season came, exactly half a century later.

Morrie Siegel, *Washington Post*

BOWL TRIPS ARE ANNUAL AFFAIRS FOR GEORGIA

In the days leading up to the 1949 Orange Bowl, which the Bulldogs would lose to Texas, the Washington Post's *Morrie Siegel wrote this article exploring the secrets to Georgia's success under Wally Butts during the 1940s.*

Football is a year-round job for Georgia coach Wally Butts, and for the last four seasons it's become practically that for his players.

Butts and his Bulldogs are here in this winter wonderland preparing for their sixth bowl appearance and their fourth in a row. Only one other football team can make that statement—Alabama.

One of the few teams able to approach that phenomenal record is Georgia's Orange Bowl foe, Texas. When the Longhorns meet the Georgians Saturday, it will be the fourth time the eyes of Texas have been on the lads from Austin on a New Year's Day game.

When Butts was installed as head coach at Georgia 10 years ago, the Red and Black football fortunes were at a low ebb. A year before, former Notre Damer Harry Mehre was dismissed in favor of Joel Hunt, who was signed to a two-year contract. Hunt was paid $9,000 not to fulfill the second year of his pact.

Butts, who was Hunt's backfield coach, was named boss this time, and Georgians are still cheering themselves over the selection.

When Butts took over the job in 1939, he said: "I'm no character builder. I'm here to win football games. If we happen to come up with a few characters on our football team, I won't object, but my principal job is to build a winning team."

Well, the little round man who two years before was a high school coach in Kentucky wasn't an overnight success. His first two Georgia productions broke even in 20 games. In 1941, however, the Bulldogs got going. They won nine and lost one and wound up in the Orange Bowl where they walloped TCU.

The next year, when a fellow named Frankie Sinkwich was a senior and another fair-to-middling footballer called Charley Trippi was a sophomore, the Bulldogs won 11 of their 12 games and spent New Year's Day in Pasadena, California, where they bumped UCLA.

Butts's overall coaching record shows 79 victories, 26 defeats, and four stalemates. Nine of those 26 losses were sustained during war years and 10 during his first two years at Georgia.

How good is Butts? Notre Dame coach Frank Leahy, recognized by fellow coaches as the "master," calls his fast friend "the best, the absolute best."

And the secret of Butts's success: for one thing, he gets tremendous help from Georgia's far-flung alumni: players like Sinkwich, Trippi, and Johnny Rauch, this year's star, just didn't happen to choose Georgia. Bulldogs standard-bearers in places like Youngstown, Ohio; Pittston, Pennsylvania; and Yeadon, Pennsylvania, put the South in their mouth.

Bulldogs Alumni Help Build Winner

Whether you're a 240-pound tackle or a 185-pound back, you've got to be fast to be on a Butts-coached team. Speed is his byword, that is speed and conditioning.

When Butts sends in a substitute, the player doesn't trot on the field—he runs at full speed. And the player he's spelling doesn't dog trot off the field—he races off also.

Next to gubernatorial foul-ups, Georgians love winning football teams. And Bulldogs alumni aim to keep it that way at Georgia. At present, they're going in for homegrown products. They recently signed up 26 Georgia-born and Georgia-bred high school footballers, most of them all-state and all-regional selections.

In case a Trippi or a Sinkwich or a Rauch comes along "up Nawth," however, they'll make room for him. Provided, of course, he can run.

Gary Pomerantz, *Washington Post*

DOOLEY: MAN IN NEED OF A FITTING IMAGE

The Bulldogs were gunning for a possible second national champi-onship as they prepared to play Penn State in the 1983 Sugar Bowl, a game they would lose 27–23. Leading up to that game, the Washington Post's *Gary Pomerantz took a close look at Coach Vince Dooley's image and his role in the team's success.*

Here he is, Vince Dooley, 19-year Georgia coach, and he has won everything but an image. The Bear has his houndstooth, Bo has his scowl, Holtz has his humor, Paterno has his professorial pugnacity.

Vince Dooley has a 151–58–6 record. And a 151–58–6 image. Only numbers. If it's true that football is religion in Georgia, it seems odd that no Bulldogs fan from Atlanta to Athens, from Savannah to Wrightsville, really knows his spiritual leader.

"I…hardly know anything about him," says Jeff Sanchez, Georgia's junior free safety.

"I'm a southerner," Dooley, 50, says. "I grew up in Alabama, coached there and in Georgia. In this country, you can't get more South than that."

Dooley is not that simple. At Auburn, where he was an All-Southeastern Conference safety and later learned the rites of football as an assistant to Ralph "Shug" Jordan, Dooley earned his master's in history.

At home, he has history books everywhere. They are about battles and generals, mainly.

"Southern politics was my interest in school," Dooley says. "I did a lot of reading on demagogues like Huey Long and Pitchfork Ben Tillman. I like history. You're affected by it."

Focus

Now history is affected by Dooley. New Year's night, number one Georgia (11–0) will play number two Penn State (10–1) for what might become Dooley's second national championship in three years. The marquee of hype reads: "Herschel Walker versus Joe Paterno."

Once again, Vince Dooley will be in the spotlight and not in the spotlight. At the same time.

Hasn't it always been this way?

"I don't particularly dislike the recognition," Dooley says. "And I don't particularly like it."

Certainly, after 19 years and only one losing season, he has an ego. "But you really never see it," says Bill Lewis, Georgia defensive coordinator.

There is a 'round-the-clock organization and dedication befitting of an ex-marine. Christmas Eve, Dooley spent four hours at the office going over defensive strategies with Lewis.

"And on Christmas Day, he went to the office twice. What for?" says Barbara Dooley, the coach's wife. "Who knows? He is never off duty. He's a perfectionist. Vince never leaves anything half done. If he was chopping down a tree, he wouldn't leave half a tree. Not even a stump."

And there is discipline, all the way to the point of no return. "Coach Dooley told us if anyone gets out of line in New Orleans," says John Lastinger, Georgia's quarterback, "they'll get a one-way bus ticket back to Athens."

"I'm more understanding now than I used to be, more tolerant," is how Dooley puts it. "Nowadays, I can look a player right in the eye, smile, and say, 'You're dismissed from the team.'"

Dooley has become so tolerant, he says of himself, he's even starting to understand and admire General Grant.

"[Vince is] not so rigid as he used to be," says Barbara Dooley. "He used to be so shy that people thought he was conceited. Really, he was just quiet."

Some say Dooley has lived in Bear Bryant's shadow. After all, he works in Bryant's conference, in Bryant's South. Dooley disagrees, saying, "I haven't coached in anyone's shadow."

It seems curious to think that the good folks of Georgia once doubted Dooley. In 1964 he left his Auburn assistant's job to become Georgia's head coach. The previous year, there had been a scandal at Georgia in which, it was rumored, Alabama's 32–7 victory over the Bulldogs was fixed. *The Saturday Evening Post* reported it. Later, it was disproven.

But Georgia football became a house divided. "I was young enough [32] not to be bothered by all that. I figured I would come in and ignore it, but the first few years were a little tough," Dooley says.

After a 7–3–1 first season, Dooley began the next year by beating Bear's 'Bama, 18–17. Later in that 1965 season (6–4), Dooley was offered the head coaching job at Oklahoma.

"I'd always admired Bud Wilkinson," Dooley says. "And it was a great offer. I almost went."

On the Georgia radio stations, Barbara Dooley remembers, they kept reading telegrams begging Dooley to stay in Dixie. "And every five minutes they played a song, asking him to stay, too," she says.

She adds, "My daughter, who was five then, came home from school and said, 'Daddy, we can't move to Oklahoma. Only Indians live there.'"

Vince Dooley stayed put. The doubts moved on.

When he was head coach at Southern California, John McKay said, "I don't coach the players, I coach the coaches."

Vince Dooley's the same way. "I hire good coaches," he says, "then I let them coach."

Every day, Dooley sits down with his assistants and discusses every player on the team. Each day, Dooley assigns a different assistant to talk to the team before practice, then he elaborates on what was said; it works almost the same way at halftime.

"He's not really a coach. He's an overseer," says Sanchez.

"A lot of football teams are unable to avoid the valleys after the peaks," says Lewis. "Georgia is able to avoid those. It's a reflection of Vince's personality. He's so consistent."

Dooley is big on motivation. Almost always, it is a motivation based on history and war.

"Every year, he tells the team the story of the Korean War where the marines were trapped in Inchon and battled out," says Wayne Radloff, senior offensive guard.

Before the Bulldogs played at Kentucky October 23, Dooley took the team to Kentucky's Spendthrift Farms to see Affirmed, a winner of the Triple Crown.

Entering this season, Georgia had won two straight SEC titles. Apparently, Dooley associated winning horse racing's Triple Crown with winning three consecutive SEC titles. Again, in history he sees relevance.

"He talked about the horse as an athlete, about the heart and the desire," says Radloff. "He talked about horses so much some of us got a little sick of hearing about them."

Result: Georgia 27, Kentucky 14.

"Growing up in Georgia, all I heard was Bear Bryant, maybe Joe Paterno," says Daniel Dooley, the second of four children and a freshman on the Georgia scout team. "I used to wonder if people compared my father with them. Now, I realize, my father has only two things in common with Bear Bryant: coaching football and winning."

"I fear him," Daniel says of his father. "I guess he's such a personal person. He never lets anyone get close. We're close as father and son. But we've never really sat down and talked, you know, about things. At first, that bothered me. But now, I understand the way he is."

This puts Daniel in the minority.

"I'd like to be a football coach someday, too," he says.

Josh Kendall, *Athens Daily News*

RICHT FINDING HIS WAY

Mark Richt took over as Georgia's 25ᵗʰ head coach for the 2001 season. The following story was written shortly after he was hired to replace Jim Donnan.

Casey Weldon wasn't sure if he was ready to get into coaching this year until he learned Mark Richt had been hired at Georgia.

"To me, he's the guy you want to be like," Weldon said. "You want to be the dad he is. You want to be the husband he is. If you're a coach, you want to be the coach he is."

Weldon called Richt to inquire about the quarterback coaching position, a job that eventually went to former Georgia player Mike Bobo. But Bobo's hiring did nothing to dampen Weldon's esteem for the man who coached him to the cusp of winning the Heisman Trophy at Florida State.

In fact, it's tough to find someone who has crossed Richt's path in the last 15 years who doesn't feel their way has been brightened by the convergence.

Weldon's mother calls Richt and his wife, Katharyn, "the most awesome people you'll ever meet."

Georgia athletics director Vince Dooley said, "He's extremely well-received for a lot of good reasons. I think everybody will go out of their way to help him succeed. Everything he needs, people want to do it because he's such a good person."

The key event in the shaping of the Mark Richt who Dooley hired as the Bulldogs' 25ᵗʰ head coach on December 26 came in 1986 when Florida State offensive lineman Pablo Lopez was killed by a gunshot at a party in Tallahassee. Seminoles head coach Bobby Bowden used the event to stress the importance of Christianity to his players.

Bowden's message hit a nerve with Richt and began his transformation from self-absorbed to self-aware.

"There's a big difference in my life now," said Richt, 40. "In 1985, I was worried about me. Basically, that was about it. The world was revolving around me and my life, and my decisions were made based on, 'How's it going to affect me?' Where now my decisions are made based on, 'What do I think God wants me to do in regard to career, family, friends, whatever?' That's the biggest difference. Before, all my concern was, 'How can I get where I want to go?' Now it's, 'Where do I think He wants me to go?'"

The change has been encompassing. On Richt's final day in Tallahassee before moving to Athens to begin full-time work at Georgia, the family said an emotional good-bye to their church family at Celebration Baptist.

"This was not a congregation member who just came to be recognized," Celebration pastor Jerry Garrard said. "It would not be unusual for Mark Richt to have coached in a very intense game the day before and work in the preschool the next morning. You'd see him sitting in there on the floor with the kids. That says a lot about what kind of man he is.

"He's just a good guy."

Most Athenians who meet Richt are first struck by his calm. He manages to be almost shy without being reclusive and reserved without being distant from his fan base. On National Signing Day, Richt and his new staff mingled among the Georgia fans gathered at the Butts-Mehre Building for half an hour in the morning, and Richt spent another half hour addressing many of the same people again that afternoon.

"Mark's great quality is meekness," said Dave Van Halanger, Georgia's strength and conditioning coach who followed Richt to Athens from Florida State, of his close friend and jogging partner. "He's very humble but has a very strong personality inside. He knows exactly what he wants, but he's not overbearing. Meek is not weak. Meek is strength. To me, meekness in Mark is great strength because he's approachable; he's humble enough to continue to learn.

"He knows that God's blessed him, he knows that people matter, he cares about people, he cares about the [players], cares about how they feel. But he knows exactly what they need. He knows you can't give them candy all the time because it will rot their teeth out."

Richt has had to spend as much time dealing with off-field discipline as on-field preparation since arriving in Athens two months ago. Four Bulldogs have been arrested, and another three have been suspended since the beginning of the year.

While the focus will return to the field this week with the opening of spring practice Tuesday, those types of off-field incidents will never be ignored, Richt insists. During his first meeting with his new team, the Boca Raton, Florida, native told the Bulldogs that winning SEC and national titles was a priority, but not the number-one priority.

"I told those guys when we first met with them that winning games is paramount and winning championships is paramount. But more than that, we want them to get their degrees, more than that we want them to be successful in life," he said. "I told them, 'If all you left here with was an SEC and a national championship ring but the rest of your life turned to crap because you didn't get your degree and you didn't know how to act and you weren't responsible, you weren't a good husband, you weren't a good father, you weren't a good employee, you weren't a good citizen—what good is that?'"

To that end, Richt will install what he calls a character-education program in the near future. "We're trying to be a little proactive about this thing, too," he said. "We're bringing in speakers to talk to these guys about right [versus] wrong. All the details aren't worked out yet, but there are a couple of people around the nation that basically will take football teams and help educate them on how to act. We want to help them."

Richt was asked several weeks ago if he thought he inherited an out-of-control program. "Not really," he said. "I know every university has its problems. If you have 18- to 22-year-old students, there are going to be problems if you take 100 players or 100 students from the general student-body population. If you tracked them through a five-year career, you're going to have some foolish things. It's just inevitable that kids are going to make mistakes."

Richt's faith has led him a tremendous distance while keeping him grounded all the while. It was during a Sunday school meeting that the Richts first thought of adopting children. Eventually they traveled to the Ukraine and adopted their two youngest children—Zack, 4, and Anya, 3. (The Richts also have two older boys—Jon, 10, and David, 6.)

Meanwhile, back at the office, Richt's inner peace allowed him to work dutifully for 15 years in the far-reaching shadow of Bowden without letting his ambition become an interfering vice.

Richt was the Seminoles offensive coordinator for the last seven years and allowed several head coaching opportunities to pass without a fight. He acknowledges that perhaps the man he used to be wouldn't have been so patient. That man might have aggressively pursued and accepted the first top job that was offered.

"That's possible, but maybe I wouldn't have been in Tallahassee. Maybe I wouldn't have done as good a job," he said. "Who knows? I don't know what could have happened or would have happened. That's hard to say."

And fruitless to contemplate. The fact is Richt waited.

"Mark was waiting for the right situation," Weldon said. "He was waiting for this."

Well, now he's got it.

The challenge from here is to build on the success former coach Jim Donnan had and to improve a team that has won 34 games and four bowl games over the last four years.

Even Garrard, thanks to his proximity to the full-blown college football fanaticism in Tallahassee and relatives in Augusta who are Bulldogs fans, understands the key to success for a Georgia football coach.

"If you don't beat Tennessee and Florida..." he said, letting the rest trail off because the implication is obvious. What he's saying is this: the sad reality is that if Mark Richt doesn't beat the Volunteers and the Gators on at least a semiregular basis, not to mention Georgia Tech and Auburn, neither his character nor his faith will save him. He still will be a good person and a respected man. He just won't be Georgia's head football coach anymore.

But those who know him have no doubts that Richt can make a smooth transition from assistant coach to head coach.

"Mark Richt is a special man," Van Halanger said. "You can just see, Mark has every great quality to be a head coach. He's learned a lot from Coach Bowden, there's no doubt about it, but Mark has his own identity."

Richt and Bowden haven't spoken since January 5, when they met in Bowden's office after Richt had cleaned out his own. There's no animosity; it's just that Richt has had his hands full making his own way and knows that his mentor has plenty on his plate, too.

"I've wanted to call him a couple of times, but I know he's busy, too," Richt said. "I didn't want to trouble him. He's got enough of his own problems, and I know Tommy [Bowden, Clemson head coach and Bobby's son] talks to him quite a bit. He probably has to hear what's going on at Clemson. I imagine [North Carolina State coach and former FSU assistant] Chuck Amato has called him from time to time. And I'll be calling. It's just the couple of times that I've thought about it, I just didn't. The times I've thought about talking to him might have been 11:00 at night, too.

"I just didn't pick it up."

Bowden was out of town this week and couldn't be reached to talk about Richt, but he made his most telling statement nine years ago. That's when he turned over complete control of his treasured offense to Richt.

"That says enough right there," said Weldon, the runner-up in the 1991 Heisman Trophy voting and now a quarterback for the XFL's Birmingham Bolts. "To have done what [Bowden] had done up until 1992 and then to turn it over and let Mark have total control of it..."

Richt proved a good caretaker. In his seven seasons as offensive coordinator, the Seminoles led the nation in scoring five times.

"He can handle [a head coaching job]," Weldon said. "He's been preparing for this since he was 22 years old."

Richt quarterbacked at Miami in the early 1980s, serving mainly as a backup for Jim Kelly, and has built his coaching reputation by molding quarterbacks. Two of his protégés—Charlie Ward and Chris Weinke—won the Heisman Trophy, and five have made NFL rosters.

"He taught me the game," Weldon said. "He's hands-on. He loves the game. He gets right in there with it. I sometimes get tired of talking Xs and Os with him."

And, still, he's learning.

"He listens, he asks questions, he's very thoughtful," Dooley said. "I feel even better now than I did when I hired him."

UGA VI sports a black jersey to honor Vince Dooley during his last home game as the school's athletic director in 2003. The long line of UGAs, which began with UGA I in 1955, is one of the proud traditions that separate Georgia football from all other programs.

Section IV
THE MYSTIQUE

Brian Curtis, *Every Week a Season*

FAITH IN THE GAME

In 2003 writer Brian Curtis visited nine different top football programs, including Georgia's, and wrote an account of a game week at each school in the book Every Week a Season. *The focus of his September experience at Georgia centers on Coach Mark Richt and the role his strong faith and spirituality play in his program.*

Number 8 Georgia versus Number 25 South Carolina
Athens, Georgia
September 7–13
This game is the SEC opener for both teams. It is a border war between two of the South's most ardent rivals. It is one of the most recognizable coaches in the University of South Carolina's (USC) history, Lou Holtz, against the young wizard, Mark Richt. Georgia enters the game highly ranked despite a sluggish win over Middle Tennessee State (MTSU) the week before. South Carolina is 2–0 after a stunning thrashing of then–number 15 Virginia. The Dawgs are led by quarterback David Greene but might play without standout Fred Gibson, injured late in the MTSU game. The Gamecocks sport an aggressive defense, but have an untested young quarterback.

It really is quite impressive. The whole thing. As you ride up one of the two glass elevators in the University of Georgia's Butts-Mehre Heritage Hall building, the headquarters of Georgia athletics, you are struck by the neon. This in a town, in a state, in a region of the country where you would least expect such showiness. There are bright red letters on the cement walls inside the elevator shaft spelling out a familiar phrase: "How 'bout them Dawgs?" If you take the elevator to the third floor, you are awestruck by the college's Hall of Fame, packed with trophies, memorabilia, flags, video highlights, and all else Georgia. If you get off the elevator on the second floor, the opening is even more dramatic, as you are thrust into the Larry Munson Trophy Room, where the 1982 Heisman Trophy that Herschel Walker won rotates on its platform. Surrounding the Heisman are dozens of bowl trophies and SEC championship statues, the national championship trophy from 1980, and engraved lists of Georgia football records, captains, and champions.

The trophy room serves as the lobby for the Georgia football offices, which looks more like a corporate suite than an athletics office. The suite is circular, with the coaching offices and film rooms lining the outer walls. As you walk around the hallway, your eyes turn to the pictures and plaques. Many former Georgia players now playing in the NFL are pictured playing with their pro teams; there are enough to cover most of the walls. There is a comprehensive list of every Georgia player who ever played in the NFL. Near the entrance sits a 10-foot-wide glass case displaying footballs with the logos of teams who drafted Bulldogs in the first round.

In short, there is no mistaking two things as you walk the hall: (1) Georgia has a heck of a lot of former players in the NFL, and (2) they are darn proud of it.

One set of doors is unlike the others in the hallway, both in texture and stature. While the assistant coaches' offices hide behind dark wood, the head coach's suite is guarded by a set of shaded glass doors. On one door, in white lettering, are the words *Head Coach*. On the other, *Mark Richt*. Take a few steps past the reception area and you are in Richt's impressive corner domain. There is an abundance of natural light, with windows dominating two walls of the office that overlooks the practice fields. A beautifully crafted conference table sits on one side of the room with four chairs. The wall to the right is covered by bookshelves that are home to many of Richt's prized possessions: pictures of his wife, Katharyn, as well as of his four children; framed writings from the Holy Bible and scriptures; and a piece of hardware acknowledging him as the 2002 SEC Coach of the Year. His desk is covered in papers, and behind him rests a flat-screen computer. A large-screen television is nearby.

It is at this desk the head coach sits on Sunday afternoon, just 24 hours after his team improved to 2–0 after a win over Middle Tennessee State. He is on the phone for the weekly SEC teleconference, answering questions from various reporters around the South. His first question is about the injury to star receiver Fred Gibson. The potential All-American injured his hamstring late in the game against MTSU on a kick return, at a time when the end result of the game was no longer in doubt. Richt indicates that he does not know the status of Gibson (he might know by Monday) and then takes blame for not pulling Gibson from the kick-return unit. He had walked over to the special teams huddle before sending them out, he explains, but never realized that Gibson was one of them. Gibson's status, it seems, will be topic number one for the week. There are other questions about what he learned from watching the MTSU game film and what he expects from South Carolina. "We need to score touchdowns," is his response in some manner to both questions. Besides cutting down on the penalties (Georgia had 18 against MTSU), Richt believes his offense must find ways to score TDs. This is imperative, he says, because in the last two games against South Carolina, Georgia has scored exactly zero offensive touchdowns.

When the teleconference ends—or, rather, when Georgia sports information director Claude Felton, listening in on his cell phone in Richt's office, puts an end to it—the tall 43-year-old puts on some running shoes and hurries out the door to meet his family for dinner. He has already been at the office for five hours, watching film from yesterday's game, talking with coaches, and poring over stats from his game and from other SEC games. He returns to the office, after dinner, at 7:00 PM to do his weekly call-in radio show. The show typically runs from 8:00 to 9:00 PM, but due to President Bush's address to the nation, it is moved up. The coaches work feverishly on Sunday night, and the men won't return to their homes until near midnight.

In the shattered land of the former Soviet Union, on soil that has been battered by war, famine, and death, sits the young nation of the Ukraine. A small town 100 miles inside the border has an orphanage, home to too many abandoned children. There are thousands of orphans in the country, and not many takers. When visitors come through, the children yell "Mama" or "Papa" to attract attention. They know the routine.

Thousands of miles away in a Sunday school class at Celebration Baptist Church in Tallahassee, Florida, the pastor and his parishioners are talking about God's will to care for others, the ills of society, how we should give back, how to be unselfish. The Bible says to take in the hungry, the poor, and the orphans. The idea resonates with some of the churchgoers—among them, Mark and Katharyn Richt.

In late 1998, Katharyn's sister-in-law made a trek to the Ukraine to adopt an orphan. She took along a video camera to capture the journey. When she returned, the Richts watched the tape and were taken with the love on the faces of the children. They already had two sons, Jon and David. Adoption is never an easy process, and it is made even more difficult when the orphanages are on the other side of the world. There was one boy on the video, Andre, who had personality and whom Katharyn's sister-in-law believed would fit right in with Jon and David. But in addition to Andre, someone else caught their atten-tion. It was a small child with blond hair and a facial deformity. It was little Anya. The Richts couldn't even decipher her gender, but their hearts and souls were drawn to her.

So in July 1999, Katharyn traveled to the Ukraine to spend time with Andre and Anya. As it turned out, Andre had been adopted by another family. During her visit, she fell in love with a second child, Ruslan (now called Zack). He was running all over the place, seemingly out of control—Katharyn figured he would fit right in with their other kids.

In late July, just a week before fall practice began, Mark Richt took a week off from his duties as offensive coordinator at Florida State and headed overseas to join his wife. He, too, was enamored with both children. After careful prayer, he and Katharyn decided to adopt them both. Richt flew back to Florida while his wife stayed behind to finalize the complex details and bring the new additions home.

Overnight, the Richt family went from four to six, but that didn't bother them. To the Richts, it was a service to God, a small gesture to help those less fortunate. "You can't just talk about wanting to save the children," Katharyn Richt said to *The Atlanta Journal-Constitution* in 2000. "You have to do your part, and this was our part." It is all part of a mission to serve God, a journey that began some 18 years ago.

Mark Richt's life changed in 1986. He was a GA [graduate assistant] at Florida State, just trying to make his mark in coaching when Pablo Lopez, an offensive tackle at FSU, was shot and killed in Tallahassee. The team and staff were shaken, especially Richt. He went into head coach Bobby Bowden's office seeking comfort. What he came away with was a new life. Richt began to study the Bible, attend church more often, and live his life in the way he believed God had envisioned. Richt became a devout Christian. Since then, his devotion to God and his job have become one. "My motivation daily is to try and honor Him by working as hard as I possibly can and succeeding in whatever I do," he says. There is no mistaking that Richt is a man of faith, from the way he carries himself to his influence on the Georgia program to his prioritization of family and his willingness to share his faith. Katharyn dedicated herself to Christ shortly after the birth of their second child. She continues her faith, not just in church, but also through weekly Bible studies with other coaches' wives.

Richt does not leave his faith at the office door. Spirituality is a big part of the Georgia football program. His brother-in-law, Kevin Hynes, serves as the team's chaplain, as an employee of the Fellowship of Christian Athletes (FCA), an international organization promoting Christianity among coaches and players at all levels. FCA leads study groups or "huddles," works with athletes and coaches to develop curriculum, and otherwise provides a spiritual aspect to sports. The book they publish, *God's Game Plan*, is part Bible, part study guide and can be found in the locker room, players' lounge, and coaches' offices. There are references to God on strength coach Dave Van Halanger's workout room walls. Rule number seven, for instance, reads, "Ask God for help." Staff meetings open with devotion, as they do at many schools. Team chapel is held on game days. Cussing and other vices are frowned upon.

All of the FCA meetings, devotions, and religious activities are voluntary, and a large number of players and coaches choose to attend.

There have been Muslims and other non-Christians on the team, and they are treated no differently. "I will not push my beliefs on anyone," Richt insists. "If they come to me, or want to accept Jesus Christ, then I will share with them. But in no way am I trying to force it on anyone." The coach's deep religious commitment came to light after a win over Auburn in 2002, when Georgia clinched the SEC title. Richt started off his postgame news conference with some surprisingly spiritual comments that made news.

Junior defensive end David Pollack admires Richt's devotion. Pollack is as devoted to God as his coach is and attempts to carry himself in the same manner. "It is very encouraging, having your coach be open about faith. That a man of God is running the program. I learn from him."

Richt's faith allows him a unique balance in life and in coaching. The minor things that may infuriate most coaches seem to roll off of Richt. He maintains a steady emotional keel in practice, during games, and away from football, which allows him to make clear decisions and focus on the task at hand. It's as if he is constantly at peace with himself and those around him, something you don't find often in football.

A native of Boca Raton, Florida, Richt headed to the University of Miami as a quarterback in 1978, but ended up playing behind future Hall of Famer Jim Kelly. After graduation in 1982, Richt latched on with the Denver Broncos, again saddled behind a Hall of Famer—John Elway. His final stop in the NFL was back home with the Miami Dolphins, where, yep, he sat behind Dan Marino. It was clear that it was time to put his playing days behind him. His first coaching job was as a GA at Florida State, under Bobby Bowden, from 1985 to 1986. He moved into the volunteer assistant slot for one year. Word spread about a talented young coach in Tallahassee, and in 1989 he became offensive coordinator at East Carolina. It was not a major program, but it was Division I, and it was almost unheard of that such a young and inexperienced coach got a coordinator position.

Richt was at East Carolina for only a year when Bowden called him back to Tallahassee, where Richt became the quarterbacks coach in 1990 and added offensive coordinator duties in 1994. He had five FSU quarterbacks move on to the NFL, including Heisman winners Chris Weinke and Charlie Ward. Florida State became a national power in the 1990s, and Richt was largely responsible. His reputation grew, and whenever a major head coaching job opened, his name was inevitably mentioned.

When it was announced that Georgia coach Jim Donnan would not be returning after Georgia's Oahu Bowl in late December, Richt set his sights on Georgia. Things began to unfold in December 1999, weeks before Florida State was to play Oklahoma for the national title in the Sugar Bowl. "Georgia was always the school that Katharyn and I envisioned ourselves at," Richt reflects. "We wanted to be in the South, and I thought it would be the SEC. Years earlier, the thought was there that FSU could be my job, but prayer and time changed that." He wanted the Georgia job so badly that he picked up the phone and called Georgia athletics director Vince Dooley to lobby. He also called Grant Teaff, the executive director of the American Football Coaches Association, and asked him to call his close friend Dooley on his behalf. When Dooley spoke with Bowden about Richt, the FSU coach had confidence in his knowledge and abilities but was concerned that Richt was "too nice."

Richt traveled with Weinke to the Heisman ceremonies in New York and met Dooley, who was in the city attending festivities for the College Football Hall of Fame. The two talked at the Waldorf-Astoria on December 11. Dooley and Georgia president Michael Adams talked in the next week with Green Bay wide receivers coach Ray Sherman and Miami Dolphins assistant Chan Gailey. Dooley and Adams flew to Tallahassee on December 19 for a second interview with Richt. Shortly after that meeting, Richt was offered the job. Surprisingly, he did not immediately accept. "I think I just got cold feet," the coach says. "It was something we had wanted and prayed about, and now it was here."

Richt asked Dooley if he could think about it and call him the next morning. After prayer and thought, he called Dooley at his home at 2:00 AM and accepted the job. Georgia did not want to make an announcement until after the Oahu Bowl, so the secret was kept until the day after Christmas as Richt prepared to coach FSU in the title game against Oklahoma.

"I knew that Georgia football was big," Richt says now. "I guess I didn't know how many demands on my time there are. I knew from watching Coach Bowden that he had a lot to do, but I learned quickly." People stop Richt at restaurants, at the gas station, or at church to say hello, wish him luck, or ask for an autograph. "The first time I realized how big Georgia football was," Katharyn Richt points out, "was when we were looking for homes and all of the cars' license plates and stickers were Georgia. There were no other schools."

Mark Schlabach has been covering Georgia football for the past 10 years, first as a student reporter for the *Red & Black* and now for *The Atlanta Journal-Constitution*. He knows what Georgia football was before Richt's arrival, and he knows what it's been like since.

"I think he [Richt] put it best when he said we need to take the lid off the program. The program had good athletes and great recruits, but they just couldn't do anything once they got to Athens." What impresses Schlabach the most about Richt is his honesty and humility. "He is willing to admit mistakes and say, 'I screwed up.'" When

Richt arrived in Athens, he brought back a sense of Georgia tradition, brought back former greats to talk to the team, and put *G*s everywhere. The sense of respect for the program is now so strong that the players, coaches, and staff will not step on the large *G*s on the carpets in Butts-Mehre.

"Coach Richt is just so grounded and humble," says defensive line coach Rodney Garner. "The kids need to feel safe, and he creates that environment for a comfortable relationship between coaches and players."

Richt's success at Georgia in his first two years, on and off the field, convinced administrators to offer the coach a new, eight-year contract, which runs through December 2010. The total package is worth between $1.5 and $2 million. His base salary is $200,000, and television and radio bring him $600,000. He has a golf club membership and two cars. He receives $400,000 for equipment endorsements and $3,600 worth of Nike shoes and apparel each year. If Richt completes the length of the contract, he receives an additional $1.6 million. Interestingly, his contract stipulates that Richt is required to make at least 12 appearances at Bulldog Clubs and spend two days helping the president fund-raise.

Every day, Georgia players are greeted in the training room by 25-year-old Mark Christiansen. An Athens native, Christiansen is a passionate Bulldogs fan, trivia master, and two-year staff member. He suffers from cerebral palsy, which has relegated him to a wheelchair and left him with little ability for physical movement. Two years ago, he wrote letters to head trainer Ron Courson and Vince Dooley asking for a job. He has it. Every day, with the help of an aide or his mother, Christiansen splits his time greeting training room visitors at Butts-Mehre and greeting guests across the street at the basketball arena. He also counts repetitions as players rehabilitate their injuries. He needs to take breaths often and sometimes loses count, but he brings a smile to those he touches and, more importantly, as Courson points out, he reminds players that their injuries pale in comparison to what others go through. It is a far cry from the splendor and pageantry that are college football.

Next door to the training room sits the newly renovated, $2.3 million players' locker room. It is so new that workers were putting the finishing touches on it right before the players reported for camp in August. There is nothing different about what is in the locker room (lockers, equipment room, players' lounge), but what sets the Georgia facilities apart is the lavish quality. The players' lounge features a large-screen television, study tables, and workstations with phones and computers. There is also an adjacent video-game room with five 32" televisions attached to Sony PlayStation and XBox games. Each is situated in front of a black leather couch. On the wall of the video room are two red LCD timers. Controlled by a switch upstairs in the coaches' suite, the clocks count down from five minutes to alert the players when meetings are about to begin. When the clocks hit 0:00, the power in the room is shut off.

There is a mailbox for each player; most currently hold a copy of *Pumped: Straight Facts for Athletes about Drugs, Supplements, and Training*. There is a message board and two computer screens that automatically post messages about meetings, practice dress, and other items for the players. The wooden lockers themselves are positioned in rows, organized by jersey number, with the player's name and number emblazoned above. The rows of lockers empty into a large carpeted area below a huge *G* that hangs from the ceiling. Eight-foot-high displays of past Georgia players who have won major awards or who have had their numbers retired surround the center area. Beyond that, on higher walls, are the names of all of Georgia's All-Americans. Near the exit to the locker room is a posting board, and this week it is covered with dozens of articles on Saturday's opponent, South Carolina.

All of the fancy and elaborate facilities in the world don't mean victories, but they do help you land players who can get you wins. And they do help those players continue on their path toward an undefeated season.

Most Monday mornings start with an 8:30 AM staff meeting in the conference room in the coaches' suite, but Vince Dooley has called a meeting of all head coaches, and Mark Richt attends. The football staff meeting finally gets under way near 10:00 AM, with 18 staff members filling the room around the large mahogany table. One wall has a video screen, while another holds a master calendar. Two opposite walls display the depth charts for Georgia and its upcoming opponent. Many of the coaches are sitting in their chairs when Richt enters, dressed in a blue collared shirt and a pair of khaki pants.

"Who has this morning's devotion?" he asks.

Every morning begins with a prayer and a short reading. The staff bow their heads as they ask for good health, continued success, and grace for their families. The injury report comes next, as described by trainer Ron Courson. Courson is a no-nonsense guy who oversees a staff of 10 and holds enormous influence over the coaches and players because of his experience. He passes out a list of injuries, then proceeds to go over the list, one player at a time. Of course, he stops for a moment at Fred Gibson. "There is no bleeding, swelling, and he was in this morning for treatment. We will let him run a bit this afternoon and take it day by day." With more than 120 players on the team, and nearly 25 of them having some sort of injury, the injury report consumes 10 minutes.

A discussion of penalties follows Courson's report. At every Monday staff meeting, secondary coach Willie Martinez goes over each penalty call from the previous game. Of course, after having committed 18 penalties on Saturday against Middle Tennessee State, there is much to discuss. Identifying the perpetrator, then giving his assessment of whether or not it was a good call, Martinez proceeds through all 18. Richt becomes engaged in the discussion, particularly on the subject of substitution penalties. "Was it my fault that we didn't get that off in time, Sir?" he inquires about a delay-of-game penalty on a punt. (All coaches and players at Georgia refer to each other as "sir"—even Richt). "Did I take too much time to make the decision, or did the players not know who was in?" In moments of self-evaluation, which are common for Richt, he takes notes on what he could do better, just as he had done the day before with the media, taking blame for having Gibson in on the play late in the game.

The meeting breaks at 11:15 AM with Richt rising to his feet and saying, "Let's go to work, men." South Carolina stampeded number 15 Virginia on Saturday, so the Georgia staff faces a formidable foe. Perhaps without their top receiver.

Every Monday night is family night—the coaching staff's families join the team for a meal on the outside deck of Butts-Mehre overlooking the practice fields. Tonight, there are crabs, chicken, vegetables, and cookies, and the players and coaches sit together under a large tent. Many of the wives and kids have shown up, and Richt enjoys the time with Katharyn and three of his kids (his oldest is at football practice). As the wives and coaches chat, kids run around throwing the football, giving players high fives, and eating more than enough cookies. As the team finishes up the meal, they head to position meetings in the first-floor meeting rooms until it is time to dress for practice.

At 7:20 PM, the players are seated on a small hill alongside one of the four practice fields. Richt begins by announcing the players who made Academic Honor Roll, based on summer class performance, as well as the recipients of Victor Club (given to players for outstanding performance by their position coach) and Dawg Bone Awards (given out for exceptional plays, including big hits, touchdowns, and interceptions). After each name is announced, the team claps once in unison.

"Men, I really don't know where we stand right now," he says, shaking his head. "We got all pumped for Clemson, played well, and, honestly, probably we were overinflated. Then we played like we did on Saturday." The players get the point. "I watched a television copy of the South Carolina game, and I tell you what—one thing that stood out was just how intense and fired up they were from the start. They not only have a good defense, I think they have a great defense. They played like it was a national championship game, and they need to, to win every one—just like we do. We need this game. We can get ourselves in a hole this season by losing early. We need a great week of practice."

With that, the team begins its warm-ups, stretching and jogging, before doing an intense running drill called fifths, where groups of players sprint around the outside of the field five times, each time after a 30-second break.

Richt has scheduled a light practice with 12 five-minute periods, and the players wear no pads, just helmets. They spend the first six periods on punts, field goals, and kickoffs. Special teams coach Jon Fabris is intense and reacts strongly when a player misses a blocking assignment. Richt stands off to the side observing, joking with some players, and talking with director of football operations Steve Greer. He is dressed in sneakers, khaki shorts, and a gray T-shirt that reads "Finish the Drill" on the back.

Periods 7–12 have the first- and second-team offenses working on scripted plays against the scout defense. The coaches want to get the offense familiar with some of the South Carolina blitzes, and they repeat running and passing plays, rotating in quarterbacks. Offensive coordinator Neil Callaway and quarterbacks coach Mike Bobo run the plays as Richt stands eight feet back, occasionally interjecting a comment. Richt's calmness contrasts with the screams of Fabris and the booming voice of defensive coordinator Brian VanGorder. "You are not listening to what I said," VanGorder shouts to a player who can't help but listen now.

Practice comes to a close around 9:10 PM, but the night is not over for the coaches—they retreat to their meeting rooms to watch film on South Carolina and continue to plan. The offensive staff leaves the office by 11:00 PM, while the defensive coaches are still hovering in the office when today becomes tomorrow.

Suffice it to say, defensive end David Pollack had a pretty good year in 2002. He had 102 tackles and 14 sacks. He was the SEC Defensive Player of the Year, a first-team All-American, and one of five finalists for the Nagurski Award, given to the nation's top defensive player. But now the secret is out. He is sure to see double-teams and extra attention from offenses.

"It is trying mentally and physically," the junior responds. "I think I am a better football player this year in terms of knowledge, technique." Much of that growth he attributes to the coaching staff, both to Richt and VanGorder. "The coaching staff puts us in a position to do well every week. They teach great fundamentals. We probably play the hardest for four quarters than anybody in football."

Pollack not only has great respect for Richt as a coach, but also as a man. He respects the fact that Richt doesn't break rules and lives by the disciplined philosophy of "my way or the highway." "He treats us as his own sons," Pollack says. "He doesn't want you to embarrass yourself or your family."

Pollack is far from an embarrassment. It shows every day in practice, in the classroom, and in life. He is a team captain, a history major in good academic standing, a man of faith who speaks to local youth groups, and a raging terror on the field.

He knows that South Carolina will double- or triple-team him. He knows Saturday will be a battle.

Tuesday is media day, and media day at Georgia is a busy one. Richt arrives at the basketball arena for his press conference, early enough to grab lunch and sit with the 25 reporters in attendance. Eating with the press is not typical for Richt, but today he has time. Following a short opening statement by the coach, the first question is not surprising: "Coach, how did Fred look?" Richt answers candidly, telling the crowd assembled that "Gibson jogged a mile last night" and that "we're being cautious." Other issues that come up include the medical condition of running back Tony Milton and the potential redshirting of running back Kregg Lumpkin. If Milton cannot play or is limited, Lumpkin will be called upon to fill in as one of three backs. If Milton is out but can play next week, wasting a redshirt year for Lumpkin will be detrimental, Richt explains. The questions and answers continue for 30 minutes, and then Richt speaks individually with writers and does six television interviews outside.

By the afternoon, the coaches have a good idea what plays they will run against South Carolina, Brian VanGorder included. Based on his assessment of his own personnel and after watching film of South Carolina, the defensive coordinator and linebackers coach knows that USC uses 11 and 12 personnel much more than 21. VanGorder passes out a 50-page scouting report on South Carolina to the linebackers and goes over a stat sheet with the seven players in his meeting. He points out that the tendency for USC is to run the ball in 12 and that when the Gamecocks face a third-and-short and the quarterback is in a shotgun, he is almost always going to run with the ball. "Bottom line, we need to be smart," he says.

He reviews game clips with the players, quizzing them as to what defensive call should be made based on the offensive alignment. A few minutes in, the mouse on the computer stops working, and shortly thereafter, the whole system shuts down. VanGorder is not happy, but he quickly moves on. Throwing around terms like Roger, Larry, Blizzard, Sky, Missile, and Rocket, the coach talks the players through various plays they can expect in the game. At 3:20 PM, the group walks to the practice field to join the entire defense for a walk-through.

Practice today is intended to be the longest and hardest of the week. It is scheduled for 20 periods, and the coaches warn the team that there will be a lot of live drills, meaning full contact and tackling. Richt walks onto the field sporting a big straw hat and the same attire as yesterday: khaki shorts, gray T-shirt, black Nike shoes. After warm-ups, the team splits into position drills and the fields fill with activity. Richt has the quarterbacks practicing snaps; Callaway has the offensive line doing pancake drills, where a group of five linemen flatten willing participants as they surge forward; the running backs work on agility; the receivers take passes; the defensive line, with coach Rodney Garner, does grunt work on dummies and on each other; the punters take turns booming kicks from one field to another.

Richt is in a good mood, and his players recognize it. He had planned on reading some South Carolina player quotes to the team at the end of practice, but he makes up some quotes supposedly from South Carolina players to get a laugh out of his guys, in particular the injured Fred Gibson, who is stretching nearby. "They said, 'Gibson? Who's he?'" Richt says, barely hiding a smirk.

As practice progresses, Richt walks around overlooking the offense, occasionally stepping in to encourage a player or to ask a coach a question. One field over, VanGorder and his staff are correcting player positioning on defense, quizzing players, giving them reminders. The practice builds from position drills to team-versus-scout drills until finally both first teams come together, working on the same things they just spent two hours doing, primarily goal line and short yardage. The clash is spirited and hard-hitting. Even in practice, pride is on the line. (Monday practice focuses on special teams, blitzes, and the run game; Tuesday is first-and-10, short yardage, and goal line; Wednesday is third-and-medium and third-and-long, as well as red zone; Thursday is review.)

"I thought the offense had an outstanding day," Richt says at the end of practice. "I don't know about the defense, but I assume they did, too. And scouts, you played great and hard, which is what we needed." He reads a response from South Carolina cornerback Dunta Robinson to a question about Gibson possibly sitting out that has been reported in *The State*, a South Carolina newspaper. "I hope that he plays, because if we end up winning and if he doesn't play, then they'll be saying, 'Well, they didn't have Fred Gibson.'"

Having finished the sandwiches they picked up from a nearby deli, the offensive coaches sit in the main conference room, the table they sit around littered with Diet Cokes and sunflower seeds. They watch film from practice, viewing plays over and over again, cracking jokes, pointing out mistakes, asking each other questions about alignments. Richt is relaxed, leaning back in his chair, eating hundreds of seeds. Ron Courson stops in and pulls up a chair to give Richt an injury update. "You know, with Fred, he ran some but it hurt a bit. I think he is probably doubtful for Saturday. We should hold him out, and you should plan on not having him." Richt has been hoping not to hear that news, but there is no sign of panic in his voice or on his face. Courson adds that it looks like running back Tony Milton has a long-term problem with buildup in his leg and will not be playing. Lumpkin is in.

The staff takes a short break after 9:00 PM, then settles in to watch South Carolina clips on third-and-medium and -long. One of the wipe boards in the conference room is now covered with plays for every situation, with a little space left for additions. Richt points out that the staff is actually ahead of a typical week's planning because they can watch only two of South Carolina's games, since they had only played two. As the season wears on, there will be longer hours of film, and the staff will typically watch the previous four games of an upcoming opponent.

Down the hall in a much smaller meeting room, VanGorder and the defensive coaches watch practice film, jotting down things that players did wrong, noting who was loafing on plays, and trying to focus after a long and tiring day. Every loaf that is marked down means more conditioning for the defense the following day. It will be another long night.

In the quarterbacks meeting on Wednesday, quarterbacks coach and former Bulldog signal-caller Mike Bobo takes David Greene, D. J. Shockley, and Joe Tereshinski through potential defenses they will face as Richt listens in. Bobo introduces two new plays that Richt & Co. designed late last night. Both are based on pro receiving routes and attack a perceived weakness in the South Carolina defense—five to seven yards past the line of scrimmage. The play is intended for third downs in the red zone and includes four receivers. They will work on the plays in practice.

At the opening of practice, Richt relays the day's schedule, including a game situation at the end of practice: 40 seconds left, ball on the 50-yard line, third-and-five, a field goal wins it, and no timeouts. Then Richt reads yet another quote, this one from South Carolina's quarterback Dondrial Pinkins: "I don't think they can score 15 points [the current point spread] the way the defense is playing right now. We feel like if we can put up at least 20 points, we have a good chance of beating them." Injured wide receiver Fred Gibson shows up with no ice or wrapping but with a green jersey on. Players who are injured and aren't ready for contact wear green instead of red or white to indicate that they are off-limits. A few minutes into practice, Gibson takes off the green. "He must have found out we are going to hold him out," Richt says with a smile. "I wonder if Ron [Courson] knows he is out here." Gibson does sit out practice, but stands with his teammates during drills, listening, pining for the chance to play.

Hundreds of yards away, on the deck outside of Richt's office, Katharyn Richt and three of her children watch practice and work on homework. Family has always been a big part of Richt's life, and now they are a big part of Georgia football. "I would like to be more of a team mom," the tall, striking brunette says, "but it is hard juggling my kids' schedules. It was a lot easier when I just had one when we were at FSU." Katharyn was, for example, quite close with former Seminole All-American Charlie Ward, and the two shared many conversations and memories. But Richt was an assistant then. Things are a bit different now that he is the head coach.

Being the wife of a football coach is not easy. "I think I was a bit naïve when we first got married about just how much time he would be gone. It really hit me when Mark was recruiting. That is from December to February. He would be gone the whole week, come home Friday nights for a few hours, and then head over to the university to work all weekend."

For the children, there are positives and negatives to being the coach's kids. On the plus side, you get great seats, get to travel to interesting places, and get to meet cool people. Of course, your father is not home much and you may have to move often.

"Mark is very good about when he walks in the door, whether I or one of the kids are up, he spends time with us," Katharyn says. Whether it is science experiments with his son or video dance lessons with his wife, he makes the time. Often, the Richt children will be around during practices or team events. "Mark and I never realized this, but former players have come back and told us how they want to have a marriage and family like us," Katharyn says. "I think it is good that we can be together in front of the players as well." The coach's appreciation for family goes beyond his children and wife, as his father lived in a converted apartment above the family's garage while his sister and brother-in-law, the team's chaplain, lived for a long time in Richt's home.

Wednesday night is spent watching more film—but this time it's the future, not the past, that the coaches have their eyes on. Georgia, like many staffs, sets aside Wednesday nights for recruiting purposes. The entire staff assembles in the conference room and watches tape on nearly 20 high school prospects. After conducting their evaluations, the coaches retreat to their offices and make calls to recruits. Often, more than one coach speaks to the same high schooler. The lifeblood of any major football program is recruiting. The best coaches, facilities, and fans don't win you games—players do.

At Georgia, Rodney Garner, the defensive line coach, coordinates recruiting. It is a year-round effort to snare the top players in the country. Signing day is in early February, and as soon as one class has been solidified—usually consisting of 20 to 30 players—the coaches immediately look ahead to high school juniors. By the time coaches are allowed on the road to evaluate prospects in May, the staff has created a list of 600 to 1,000 potential juniors to consider. They take recommendations from high school coaches they trust and from recruiting services. After the May travels, which at Georgia means a visit to every high school in the state, as many as six or seven visits a day, the staff whittles the list down to a "manageable" 300. It takes time, but it's clearly worth it: 81 percent of Georgia's current players are from the Peach State. Players can make unofficial visits (visits they pay for themselves) during the fall on home-game weekends; the Dawgs may host anywhere from 40 to 60 recruits, as well as parents and coaches, on unofficial visits.

The official visit in December is another story. Schools are allowed a maximum of 56 official visits a year, but some years they offer less. Last season at Georgia, only 38 players took an official visit; of those, 24 committed. The Bulldogs try to have no more than 15 recruits on an official visit on the same weekend, preferring more intimate gatherings.

On a typical official visit to Georgia, the recruit and his parents arrive in Athens around 5:00 PM on Friday and are welcomed at the Georgia Center Hotel by the Georgia Guys & Gals, the student support group for recruiting. There is a hospitality suite set up, and the players' rooms are decorated with Bulldogs paraphernalia. Friday night, dinner for the players, parents, and coaches is at the Athens Country Club, followed by dessert at Richt's home, just minutes outside of Athens. The recruits and their hosts will then head out to a party while the parents return to the Georgia Center. Saturday morning, the wake-up call comes early. The guests are taken on a tour of the campus and the new academic center, where they meet with a professor in their area of interest. They will have lunch with a professor and then head to Butts-Mehre to watch a highlight tape and tour the weight room, locker room, and meeting rooms. At 6:30, they are taken to mammoth, 92,000-seat Sanford Stadium. They are given Georgia jerseys with their names and numbers on them and are introduced on the PA system, then given free reign to run around on the field. They walk up to the SkySuites in the stadium for dinner. By Sunday morning, the recruits and their parents are exhausted, but will meet with their position coaches and Richt before heading home.

Recruiting is a high-stakes competition and is one reason why Georgia is favored to win the SEC this year. Of course, Lou Holtz and

South Carolina have some pretty good players, too, and they've proven it in the first two games of the season.

After devoting Wednesday night to the future, it is back to the present on Thursday. Richt is in the offensive-line meeting room at 2:00 PM, but seated in front of him are all of his seniors on the team, not just the O-linemen. They aren't watching film or talking about football. They are discussing the characteristics of leaders, having read a chapter from John Maxwell's *The 21 Indisputable Traits of a Leader*. The coach is teaching his weekly class on leadership, while Brian VanGorder is talking with the underclassmen about teamwork. It is all part of a development program at Georgia that Richt installed last year. Led by former NFL, college, and high school coach Bob Lankford, the character and leadership curriculum is intended to last throughout a player's years at the university.

Lankford is the CEO of Coach's Corner, an organization seeking to develop athletes mentally, physically, and spiritually. Lankford and strength coach Dave Van Halanger talk to the freshmen for 15 minutes after 6:00 AM lifting sessions on Monday and Wednesday mornings. The topics range from date rape to cheating on tests to treating teammates with respect. The curriculum was designed by Dr. Sharon Stoll, the director of the Center for Ethical Theory and Honor in Competition and Sport, based at the University of Idaho. The first year of the program is focused on "Winning in Life"; the second, "Fellowship, Followership, and Leadership"; the third year, "Decision-Making and Principled Thinking'; and the fourth year, "Men of Character in Application."

So there Richt is, sitting in a chair facing his seniors, talking about the topic for the week: generosity. After a review of the assigned story, Richt begins a dialogue of what it means to be generous, how we value giving, and why it is important. His players are not shy about sharing their personal feelings and stories. One speaks of giving his time to the rec center in his old neighborhood because most of the young kids don't have any role models. Another talks about how he often does not put others first, especially in the competitive sport of football, where it is survival of the fittest. The coach is candid as well, contributing insights from his marriage and his life as a young student-athlete.

Character is critical to everything that Richt is trying to accomplish at Georgia. That is why when his men misstep—and they do at times—it eats at him. When nine of his players were caught selling their SEC championship rings in the spring, the coach was more hurt and saddened than angry. He acknowledges that with more than 100 young men, there will be incidents. But that's exactly why they need character-building activities.

There is more self-reflection by the players on Thursday, in the wide receivers meeting with Coach John Eason. Eason reviews a weekly test, 37 questions about formations, pass routes, the game plan. And then a few other questions, like, "When did you last tell your mother that you love her?" and "Who would you give your game ball to?" Between jokes and cutups and some serious talk about pass routes, the players share their stories of growing up, how much their mother or grandmother means to them, and who they cherish the most. The room falls silent when Fred Gibson talks about giving the game ball to his grandmother, who raised him because he never met his father and his mother gave birth to him when she was just 13.

"This is where the SEC championship begins," says Richt in his prepractice talk. "It's going to be tough to lose this game and still win the championship."

The players are not in pads, as this will be a short practice: just 15 periods, no contact. David Greene looks sharp and is in a good mood. Gibson is on the field running pass patterns at full speed and starting with the first team. He believes he can play and is trying to convince the coaches. It is a far cry from the prognosis on Monday.

After the easy workout, Richt leaves his players with this thought: "You know, men, we really have not been tested since Michael Johnson's catch against Auburn [in November 2002 to win the SEC]. It might be a battle on Saturday; we might be behind and have to come back. That's when we'll know what we are."

In a town that has a bar called Gator Hater and more Georgia *G* emblems than one can fathom, football is king. And those entrusted with the 100-year tradition are the most celebrated—and sometimes vilified—public figures in the state. How big is Georgia football? The school just spent $25 million to add 6,000 seats and 20 luxury boxes to Sanford Stadium, bringing the capacity to 92,000. The football program brought in more than $35 million in revenue in 2002, with ticket sales alone bringing in close to $12.8 million. By contrast, the entire athletics department budget was $45 million. Included in the football budget are $25,000 for laundry, $485,000 for recruiting, and $15,000 for the preseason coaches' retreat. Playing in the BCS Sugar Bowl in January added $2.8 million to the coffers, and playing in the SEC championship game contributed $1 million more. Georgia football is big business. And no day is better for business than game day.

By 7:00 AM on Saturday, the tailgating has begun. All over campus—on sidewalks, on grass, in parking lots—Georgia fans have pitched tents, hoisted their flags, and started grilling food and drinking beer. The roads become clogged as the morning progresses, and the conversations and music grow louder. Richt is in his office early enough to do his pregame radio interview with Loran Smith at 10:30 AM. The players have not yet returned from Lake Elsinore, a resort 50 miles northwest of Athens where the team stays the nights before home games. (Richt joined them last night for dinner and for a brief pep talk before driving back to Athens.) Recruits begin to show up at Butts-Mehre with their parents and coaches and are greeted by the Georgia Guys & Gals, who are dressed in black skirts or pants and red and black striped sweaters.

After the players arrive and dress at Butts-Mehre, Athens swells around the team buses as they make their way across campus. They stop short of the stadium, and the players and assistants get off. It is time for the Dawg Walk. Imagine a movie premiere's red carpet, with photographers and fans screaming as stars walk down the carpet. Now multiply that by 1,000, and you're getting close. It is a decades-old tradition, and the Georgia band, cheerleaders, fans, and police line the route. The path is at first blocked off by barricades, but as you approach the stadium, it becomes a human tunnel barely two feet wide. If you can't get pumped after that walk, good luck.

Unlike just about everything else around it, the locker room at Sanford Stadium is not impressive. It is a large room with white walls, a red carpet with a Georgia G, a few dozen folding chairs. There are easel boards for position meetings, a small training room, a coaches' room. Since the team does not get dressed here, little is needed. Hanging above the door to the field is a tattered sign that reads: "Be worthy as you run upon this hallowed sod, for you dare to tread where champions have trod." After warm-ups, all of the players gather in the small shower area and get quiet. A manager turns off the lights. A player begins a prayer. "If God is with us, then who can be against us?" the group says in unison. The lights come back on, and the team takes a knee around Richt.

"We had a great week of practice. A great night last night, and today I can tell you are focused. You are ready to play. You need to out-hit, out-hustle, and out-heart them today, because I know they will be fired up."

But he doesn't have to say much. The team knows what it must do.

On the first offensive series, David Greene leads the Bulldogs down the field. Michael Cooper picks up where he left off last week against Middle Tennessee State, breaking away for a huge run into South Carolina territory on the fifth play from scrimmage. Georgia gets to the red zone, hungry for their first offensive touchdown in their last 11 quarters against the Gamecocks, and Greene finds receiver Reggie Brown for a TD. Wait. A flag on the play. An illegal formation penalty is called on Georgia and the touchdown is negated. After the team committed 18 penalties the week before, Richt and his staff have emphasized discipline all week. This is not a good start. The South Carolina defense steps up and holds Georgia to a field goal.

The Georgia defense plays strong on USC's first possession, forcing them to punt. But Lou Holtz pulls a fast one, calling for a fake punt that results in a first down.

The defense digs in, and South Carolina goes nowhere. After the series, on the bench, Brian VanGorder sits between his players, diagramming plays, offering them encouragement. On the field, Greene faces a third-and-long deep in Georgia's own territory. Split wide to his right is Fred Gibson, who, despite reports to the contrary, is ready to play. Gibson breaks free of his defender after a cut into the middle and holds on to Greene's pass as he is hit hard. The catch gets Georgia a first down, but costs them much more. Gibson does not get up. Ron Courson and his staff run onto the field as the crowd grows silent. Gibson is helped to his feet and limps off the field, takes a seat on the bench, and never returns. The hamstring injury that he had suffered the week before, the subject of so much speculation, apparently has not healed. Yesterday, after learning that Gibson could go, Richt reflected, "I hope he is ready. If he gets hurt again I will feel real bad."

Greene continues to engineer on the impressive drive, and this time, the end result is a touchdown. Reggie Brown hauls in the score over Dunta Robinson. The drought is over.

The Bulldogs defense forces USC quarterback Dondrial Pinkins—the same Pinkins who said David Pollack would "not be a factor"—into scrambles and bad passes. Pollack is double- and triple-teamed but does manage to pressure Pinkins on numerous occasions. Georgia intercepts Pinkins late in the first quarter, but at the end of the play, a Georgia player is called for a personal foul, backing them up 15 yards. Another dumb penalty. On the sideline, Richt shakes his head and breaks a small grin. It doesn't really matter, as the Georgia drive goes nowhere.

Early in the second quarter, Richt puts quarterback D. J. Shockley in the game for a series, as he's hinted he might, but on Shockley's second play, what should have been an option shovel pass to the tailback ends up on the ground, and South Carolina recovers the ball. It is Georgia's first turnover of the year. Late in the first half, Greene hits Brown again, this time on a five-yard touchdown pass. At halftime, the score is 17–0, and the crowd roars their approval.

"We cannot let up," Richt implores the team after the position coaches have met with their men. "I heard someone say that the score was 0–0. Well, *it is* 0–0. Football is a 60-minute game, not 30 minutes. I know that they have a lot of pride and will come out strong. They could score a touchdown and now it's 17–7 and they are right back in it. Maybe they take the lead. We have to stay focused and battle back."

But the second half is more Georgia—on both sides of the ball. The defense forces another turnover as Sean Jones gets his second pick of the day. Pollack is all over the place, throwing larger offensive linemen out of the way. Michael Cooper rushes for a two-yard touchdown to make the score 24–0, and in the fourth quarter, Richt begins to rest the starters. South Carolina misses a field-goal attempt, but against the Bulldogs reserves, they do manage a late touchdown. On the ensuing onside kick, Bulldogs receiver Damien Gary scoops up the ball and returns it 44 yards for a touchdown. The rout is complete, the final score 31–7. Greene finishes 16 of 27 for 208 yards, Brown catches seven passes for 104 yards and two touchdowns, and Cooper has 14 carries for 82 yards.

In the jubilant locker room, which is crowded with former players and coaches' kids, Richt praises the team. "Boy, we looked great out there today. Offense, defense, the special team coverage—we looked real good. I think we have something real special here, men. Don't you?"

The team responds with an emphatic "Yes, Sir!"

Mark Richt manages a typical week in the coaching life with an impressive resolve and strong belief in who he is and what he is doing. The setbacks do not drain him, and the successes do not change him. He has learned to be the CEO of a major college program without having to give up being a coach or being a good man. If he turns out young men of character and loyalty with a devotion to family, then he has succeeded. Winning a few football games is just a bonus.

The win for Georgia was a rout, but not all teams are on the winning side of lopsided games. Just ask Tom O'Brien at Boston College.

Matt Fulks, *Sportcaster's Dozen*

LARRY MUNSON

*One of Georgia's most beloved figures is announcer Larry Munson. In his
entry in Matt Fulks's* The Sportscaster's Dozen, *published in 1998, "the
Voice of the Bulldogs" reflects on his years behind the mike.*

Vince Dooley was an outstanding football coach for the Bulldogs. He
coached from 1964 to 1988. When he became head coach, the big wave
of commercialism, endorsements, raising money, and being on bill-
boards was just starting. I saw him going through all of that just as I got
to Georgia. He started making more and more speeches. Not to imply
that I was old and he was young, because we were both almost the
same age, but he came just as the whole industry changed.

Even now, head coaches do very little coaching. The staff does
almost all of it, and most coaches use the guys up in the booth during
the game or on headsets who call in all the plays and do everything,
and the head coach doesn't even make substitutions on the sideline.
All of that was starting when Dooley took over as head coach.

He was a self-disciplined man; he could control his temper and
not blow at anybody. He had everybody's respect. That's true even to
this day. He's athletics director now, and the people around act like he's
going to crack a whip, but he's not going to do that.

He was really a football man; he really wanted to run the ball. I've
looked back at that first book he ever wrote and am just amazed at the
diagrams of those running plays that he had in that book. It's what he
believed in. He took Georgia right out of the bottom of the tub. In 1965
he took the Bulldogs to Ann Arbor, Michigan, and Georgia beat the
Wolverines, 15–7. It was the first and only time Georgia has won up
there. Nobody ever thought they'd win that game. That win helped
people believe that Dooley was going to be a great coach.

Since I've never lived in Athens, I've never had a real close relationship with these coaches, but Dooley and I were pretty close. For
about seven years, I had a roundtable talk show in Athens on Tuesday
nights. When I went to town for that on Tuesday afternoon, I would get
to see practice, which was a first for me. When he saw me coming to
the practice field and the assistants were running everything, he would

start walking away and wait for me to come join him. We would then walk by ourselves around those practice fields. If somebody had just gotten hurt or if there was going to be some big change that week, he would tell me what was going on. If he had some worry about a player who had just flunked a test and that was occupying his mind, he'd tell me about it. I never used it on the air, but we were close enough that he could tell me about it. At night we would eat dinner at Dooley's house.

The thing that got difficult for Dooley was the various things he had to do outside of coaching. There were demands on his time from quarterback clubs and booster clubs, which started in the 1960s. At first, it wasn't bad because there weren't a lot of those clubs. All of a sudden, they ran wild as one was put in almost every town around the state. Some members of Dooley's staff, like Loran Smith and Dan Magill, got some of the Bulldog Clubs started. Once these clubs were established, they wanted Dooley to come and speak. He did, but it was very demanding on him.

Dooley did a great job for the program over the years, as he finished his coaching career with a 201–77–10 record. With Dooley, the Bulldogs also won one national championship and six SEC titles.

Succeeding a Legend

Ray Goff came in after Dooley and was very, very suspicious of the media during his first year. He thought people were out to nail him. Goff was hired for one main reason...his recruiting ability. He had been head of recruiting for Dooley. He was hired as a recruiter, and he let his assistants do virtually all the work, while he did, maybe, more public appearances than Dooley did.

There were some wild rumors, scandal, and scuttlebutt that started almost immediately when Goff started. Nobody knew if it was true or not true. Unfortunately that's about the time talk radio was also really taking off in the 1980s. Talk radio was repeating stuff without checking on it, but nobody knew. I was listening one day to a talk station in this city, and I heard the guys that morning say that Ray's wife was going to file for divorce that very morning at 8:30 in the courthouse in Athens, Georgia. The station had sent a reporting team to the courthouse in Athens. They had talked themselves into believing what they were hearing. Of course, she didn't file for divorce. There wasn't any reason for anybody to be at the courthouse, but by gosh, they were, and they spread that story. Goff had to fight that off.

Immediately, under Goff, the team was struggling. We had to screen calls during his Sunday night call-in show. When some guy would call really angry because Georgia had just lost, let's say, we tried to protect Goff. If a guy tipped his hand to you that he was going really go after Ray, the producers would screen him off, put him on hold, and take another call. To some fans, Goff couldn't replace Dooley, and they weren't going to give him a chance to keep the team at the same level where Dooley had it.

Keep in mind, now, they changed all the academic rules at the school just as Dooley went out and Goff came in. He was hurt by a real change in the academic structure at the university. There was another change three years later that hit him right after he had beaten Ohio State in the 1993 Citrus Bowl. Goff was a victim of the drastic changes and the academic rules. It took him about two years to realize that all of us at WSB were his friends. We weren't out to get him. Some of us were doing talk radio, but we weren't the Atlanta station that was after him.

Goff had a good staff that recruited and coached well. He recruited two great classes when he was the head coach. One of those classes included players like Eric Zeier, Garrison Hearst, Andre Hastings, Brice Hunter, and Randall Godfrey. He also had a great bunch of players left here when he was fired in 1995—Mike Bobo, Hines Ward, and Robert Edwards. That group finished out their careers in 1997. In his seven seasons as head coach, the Bulldogs went 46–34–1, with four bowl appearances.

In came Jim Donnan as a replacement in 1996.

Donnan is a little bit more like a throwback. He calls his own plays, for one thing, which very few coaches do. During his second season, he cut back on speeches, fund-raising, and things like that. He really wanted to get out of that. He had done whatever they asked him to do during his first year, but after that he turned it around and walked away from a lot of it. Coaches nowadays really have to do a lot of that stuff. They don't turn down any TV interviews because they really try to cooperate with the press. That's great for us in the media, but it takes a toll on the coaches.

The Georgia Bulldog

Herschel Walker, who came in under Dooley, was a great running back. There had been a violent recruiting war over Walker, with everybody accusing everybody. Clemson stayed right in to the end with us. There were all sorts of stories about money attempting to change hands.

I was doing a live television talk show on Atlanta's Channel 36 at 6:30 at night, before Herschel had signed. The recruiting's over for everybody except Herschel Walker. The decision was between Georgia and Clemson. We had a caller who was extremely excited; it was a desk clerk from a hotel in Macon, Georgia. He said that John Robinson, head coach of Southern Cal, had just checked into this hotel and was in town to sign Herschel Walker. Naturally, I believed this phone call.

There was a John Robinson who had checked in, but this desk clerk just added the Southern Cal part. He had seen the John Robinson name with "paint salesman" written under his name. Southern Cal had been in the picture about a month earlier but had dropped out. Of course, it wasn't John Robinson the coach, and the Bulldogs got Walker.

Walker helped lead the University of Georgia to a remarkable 1981 season and a national championship. There'll probably never be another year like that one. We'll never know how good that team would have been because we had a couple of very good receivers on the team, but with Walker, the other guys didn't touch the ball a lot. We had a good tight end and a quarterback, Buck Belue, who could throw the ball.

The exciting thing about Herschel was the fact that as the team came out of the huddle, especially in his freshman year, you figured he might go 75 yards. He was always breaking a long run during his freshman year; every week he broke at least one and sometimes two. By the time they got to the end of the season in 1980, other teams realized we weren't going to throw the ball at all, and hardly anybody else was even going to touch the ball other than Walker. The defenses started crowding up in the middle and bringing the linebackers up in the line, which meant we were looking at eight-man fronts.

During his freshman year, Herschel had 1,616 yards with 15 touchdowns. After that season, he rarely had another really long run in the rest of his college career, yet he gained more yardage and scored more touchdowns in his second and third years than he had in that freshman year with all the long runs. Defenses were stacked in there and pounding him to death.

His body, one day after a Florida game in Jacksonville, was covered with bruises that you could easily see. The coaches counted 24 bruises on his body, and when they looked back at the film, there were almost 24 late hits where people were sticking their head gears into him even though the whistle had blown. He had a specially designed set of pads that went all the way down to his waist, to cover all of his ribs, because people were really sticking him and trying to hurt him.

Bulldogs Tradition

There have been so many great football players at Georgia, but the guys that stick out in my mind are players who people have probably forgotten about. Glynn Harrison, for instance, was a brilliant running back from 1973 to 1975. He had a different style; he was so smooth and had deceptive moves. Jimmy Poulos, the "Golden Greek," was kind of a small running back before Harrison, but he had moves, too. Quarterback Matt Robinson, who saved us a couple of times in the mid-1970s. There have just been so many great players over the years.

All of Dooley's fullbacks used to be great blockers. We used to run sweeps with the fullback leading the way. We also used to have outstanding linebackers, a lot of whom came from north Florida. We used to raid Jacksonville heavily for players. Strangely, even though these were really tough kids who could play hurt and who made a lot of tackles, the Bulldogs never had a linebacker who made it in the NFL. Once Clemson moved into Jacksonville and shut that recruiting down, we weren't getting any more linebackers out of north Florida.

Dooley's defensive coordinator, Erk Russell, was great to watch. Players just worshipped him. He used to tell me that real quietly at the beginning of every spring practice. Dooley took the biggest kids and put them in the offensive line, regardless of where they played in high school. Dooley knew that's where everything was going to be won or lost with his running attack. He wanted to have the biggest offensive line that was possible to build. Doing that left Erk with what he called "the runts." He used to be really upset about it. He wasn't cursing about it, but he said all the size is on that offensive line. "Muns," he'd say, "all I got are these little guys." He did all right with those "little guys."

The Victory Cigar

For a long time, the victory cigar was a superstitious thing with our football broadcasts. Years ago, the engineer of the broadcast and I would light a cigar up if the Bulldogs had a lead in the fourth quarter and were managing to keep that lead. In the beginning, it wasn't necessarily a victory cigar. We never lit one up, though, unless we were actually ahead.

We forgot about it for a while because a lot of places killed smoking in the press box. We did break it out one time during the 1997 season. It was against the Florida Gators in Jacksonville. The Bulldogs led most of the game. With about 2:30 left in the game, our current producer, Larry England, who can't stand smoking, told me to light one up. Even though he wasn't with us originally, he knew we used to smoke one when we were leading toward the end of a game. That was the first time in a long time that we lit up in the press box.

It was great for me when we could light up in the press box because I love a good cigar. I don't really have a favorite brand; I smoke anything and everything. There are so many good ones out there, and people just send me boxes. I've always got some around.

Larry Munson Day

In 1997 the state had Larry Munson Day at the Georgia capitol. It was neat to go up there and to speak in front of all those guys. I looked up in the balcony and a lot of the Georgia fans were up there; and the guy that I was working with in the afternoon, Jeff Van Note, was sitting up there. I was allowed to take seven people up on stage with me. I tricked my spotter, Dick Payne, who's been with me more than 30 years, that he had to talk 60 seconds, that's all he had to do, one minute. He said, "No."

I said, "Only one minute. You can say something for one minute."

He walked up to that microphone, put his hands on each side of the podium like somebody who's made a lot of speeches (which he hadn't done), and the first words out of his mouth were, "Well, geez." Then he talked for one minute and pulled out of there.

I will always remember that distinctly.

Not everyone was happy about it, though. A nonfan, in *The Atlanta Journal-Constitution* newspaper's "Vent" column, took a crack at me by saying that having me honored by the Georgia legislature was like having former Atlanta Falcons quarterback Jeff George honored. (George is not a fan-favorite in Atlanta.) They really took a nasty crack at it.

Things like that can bother me when they're unjust or untrue. If I know it's unjust or untrue, if I hear somebody lying, like a talk show guy, it really gets under my skin—if it's totally unfair. I've never been able to stand anything like that. That bothers me.

Somebody saying that I should be compared with that particular quarterback, who at that time had a lot of enemies among the fans and the writers, didn't bother me, but the guy was obviously taking a lick at me.

It's really nice to be honored like that by the state of Georgia, and it's certainly something to be proud of from my career. But there's not really a lot of career achievements that stick out to me. I'm more proud of the fact that over the years I've been able to do a lot for children. I've adopted children and have helped raise some nieces and nephews.

I was married for a combined 46 years to two different women, 24 with one and 22 with the other, so there had to be something right in those marriages to go that long. Now that I'm older, I can contribute small amounts of money to various causes. I have two wolves in Yellowstone Park and two buffalos in Oklahoma and am contributing to the Tall Grass Prairie in Oklahoma. All of a sudden I don't want to kill geese anymore, or anything like that. I've killed geese and ducks by the thousands during my life because I used to love to do it, but now it's not as important to me.

I don't know that I've really accomplished much at all in my career. The Georgia fans are very excitable, but the whole business of radio and college athletics has changed. Cable television has changed everything. When we were all real young, to be one of the network television announcers and do a football game on a Saturday afternoon would have been a big thing. Now it doesn't mean as much. There must be 200 guys doing football play-by-play on television. If you count all the games every Saturday on all the stations, there's 14 games, and they start at 11:30 in the morning and they don't quit until 2:00 on Sunday morning. Cable has changed everything, and it's eventually going to eat everything up.

Vince Dooley with Blake Giles,
Tales from the 1980 Bulldogs

1980: THE PIG

In his book Tales from the 1980 Bulldogs, *the legendary Vince Dooley recalls how an incident involving several players and a stolen pig turned into one of the turning points of that championship season.*

The Starting Point...Sort Of

The road to the national championship might have started with a discipline problem that took place after spring practice.

The 1980 team became the ultimate team. Every year the staff talked about a point of emphasis, and competing as a team was one of the things we talked about that year. And out of that, Coach Erk Russell came up with the "TEAM me" shirts that everyone wore.

"Every new year is new life and a new start," Erk said. "But just point-blank, there was nothing that led me to believe that we were going to win 12 games that season. That's just putting it bluntly. Except we had emphasized team that spring."

Every day we talked about being a team, unselfish play, and "the team wins and everybody benefits." Each coach would get up there on a given day and give his idea of what it meant and talk about it. Putting it all together was how Erk dreamed up those shirts: "TEAM me." Now you see them everywhere.

Erk was always a gimmick guy.

"Yes," Erk said, "every year I would go see Woody Chastain at his sporting-goods store with some idea for a T-shirt. I remember he said that it was awful we don't have good enough players to win without all this crap. I saw Woody recently. I reminded him we did the 'TEAM me' shirts, and if he had been smart enough to trademark those shirts, he would have been a millionaire. Of course, I guess he is a millionaire, but he would have been a multimillionaire."

Tim Morrison, an offensive lineman in 1980, still has his shirt. His 12-year-old son wears it.

So we had really emphasized the team aspect. But there is no doubt that the purloined pig party was a factor in helping the unification of the team.

It started with a tradition the players had, which was called Seagraves. It was a spring tradition they kept to celebrate the end of spring practice.

It was a private party for the team, no coaches allowed. They always drank a lot of beer, but this year they decided to add food to the party. And that proved to be the beginning of trouble for five of our seniors. The whole team participated in the party, but just five of them got caught.

It Seemed Like a Good Idea

I have learned bits and pieces of the story over the years. But I learned pretty quickly the main facts.

First of all, the guilty players were all seniors, cornerback Scott Woerner, rover Chris Welton, and linebacker Frank Ros from the defense and two offensive linemen, Nat Hudson and Hugh Nall. Welton, the man who has the photographic memory, said he doesn't remember who dreamed up the idea. Ros, our captain in 1980, said he got the idea from the wrestling team.

"I got with Woerner, and we decided we ought to have the best Seagraves ever," Ros explained. "We wanted to do something unique. We didn't have any money to buy food. We had known that the wrestlers had obtained a sow through unorthodox means at the research center. At that age you don't think of any repercussions."

The mastermind?

"You are talking to him," said Woerner, who was an All-American cornerback in 1980. "I knew where we were going to get the pig. I had—what do you call it?—cased the joint a couple of times. I used to go to the Botanical Gardens all the time. It was a neat place for me to hang out, and the hog farm was right next to it. There was a place you could park your car. They had the big hog pens right next to where you could pull up on the road."

"We didn't mean any harm to the people at the swine research center," stated Nall, who was one of the starting centers. "It was just a fun deal that for whatever reason we decided to go that route. We probably could have had any pig farmer in the state of Georgia give us a pig, but once again we were just trying to have the best Seagraves party that had ever been. Prior to that it had always been just beverages with no food. We were going to make sure that we had food provided for our teammates."

Nall ended up being the triggerman.

"I was the one with the bow and arrow," he said. "I'm an avid outdoorsman. I had done it since high school, but only a little bit since I had been in college."

"Hugh didn't take much convincing," Woerner added with a laugh.

Hudson, a big offensive lineman, was recruited because he had some experience barbecuing hogs. Defensive end Pat McShea might have been in on the caper except that he was out with his girlfriend. Offensive guard Tim Morrison was invited, but he chose to stay home with his wife.

The Procuring

The UGA farm is just a short drive, less than three miles, from the athletics dorm. So it was a quick trip for the five Bulldogs late that night to the pigpens.

Woerner held his flashlight while Nall took aim. Hudson was standing by with a blanket.

"When you are shooting something in a 100-foot pen, it is not like you have to wait for it to come by," Woerner said. Nall hit the pig with his first shot, but it was not fatal.

"The first time he shot him, he hit him a little too far back," Woerner remembered, "and he was running down that hog wire fence. The arrow sounded like somebody put baseball cards between the spokes of a bicycle."

"The first one hit him in the shoulder blade and didn't go into him," Nall echoed. "The pig turned and walked—I can hear him right now—and walked down the fence, and the arrow sounded like those old baseball cards you used to put in the spokes of your bicycle. He was trying to get away from us.

"Hudson was there with a blanket ready to jump on him. I got around to make my second shot, and I angled it in behind the shoulder blade. It was a good hit, and I saw it penetrate, and the pig jumped, it looked like 10 feet in the air. It hit the ground, and Hudson was on top of him with that blanket to keep him from squealing. I think he had done that kind of thing before."

"He jumped straight up," Woerner confirmed. "I never thought a 400-pound hog could jump up in the air like that. It was pretty amazing."

The pig proved more adept at self-elevation than the five players did at lifting him over the fence.

"Have you ever tried to pick up a 400-pound sow?" Woerner asked. "We couldn't get it over the fence."

"The sow was huge," Ros recalled. "The five of us couldn't pick the thing up. We were strong, but we had to gut the thing in the field to get it out. That was comical."

"I don't think we did the best selection," Nall opined. "The smaller one would have been better. Once she was down, we couldn't move her. It was supposed to be one of those things where we picked her up and threw her in the back of the car. We had to field dress the pig right there to lighten the load, and once we got her to the fence, we had to prop her on the fence."

"We leaned it up against the fence and flipped it over," Woerner explained.

"It was a real stout fence," Nall added.

A Close Call

The getaway vehicle was an Oldsmobile Toronado. The slain hog was finally hoisted into the trunk for transport to Poss's Lakeview, a banquet facility owned by Bob Poss, a Bulldog letterman from the early 1940s who had the concession contract at Georgia football games and owned a catering business. On the way to Poss's, however, the players stopped at a gas station.

"We pulled in for some gas," Ros recalled. "Here are four white guys and a big black guy, and he had a cook's outfit on. He was muddy from trying to get the pig out. He was covered in mud and blood. We had a tarp on the pig, but the tarp blew over just as a cop was coming down Baxter. He did not stop. I never figured that out."

Defensive end Robert Miles remembered Hudson, his roommate, coming back to the room, covered in blood.

"What happened?" Miles asked.

"Hog blood," Hudson replied succinctly. "Hog blood."

The Cooking

Hudson barbecued the pig that night using a chain-link fence gate as a grill.

"Nat knew how to do it because he grew up doing it," Ros said. "He cooked it all night:'

"I think Nat had something he was swabbing on the pig," Nall added. "I know he had a big stick with a rag on the end of it. He was the head cook."

Woerner pronounced the party a grand success.

"There were 127 cases of beer and eight kegs," he said. "We had about 20 or 25 cases left, and when we had to hang around later that spring, it got us through."

What went on at the party was standard fraternity fare. The upperclassmen mounted the head on a stick and made freshmen kiss its snout.

Caught!

The whole episode might have gone undetected except for some careless actions by some of those freshmen.

"The older guys went back to the dorm," Welton said, "and the freshmen who had been initiated got the bright idea to cut the head down.

They threw it in the back of a truck, and they went driving around campus and dumped it on the steps of one of the high-rise dorms."

What happened out there among the team normally always stayed with the team. But then a couple of them made it public. There were a couple of students smooching, and they dropped the carcass at the couple's feet. It scared the girl to death, but the boy got the license number of the player's truck.

The Fallout

Hitch Hullis, a walk-on from Athens who had just recently earned a scholarship on the field, was the driver. Originally he was the one kid who got in trouble because it was his truck. But that bothered Ros.

"He didn't steal the pig. I went to Scott and said, 'It is not right,'" he confessed.

Woerner was watching the NCAA tennis tournament on our campus when Ros found him with the news that Hullis had been caught.

"You have got to turn yourself in," Ros told him.

Woerner said he didn't see any reason to do that, but it didn't really matter because I already had his name. I don't remember exactly how I found out about it, but I do remember calling the faculty member who was in charge. The pig was his responsibility. I was trying to tell him how upset I was and that I assured him that it would be repaid and that I would discipline the players.

And then I remember making a statement that as soon as I made it, I knew I had said the wrong thing. I told him, "I know this will be hard to believe, but these are five of the finest individuals I have on the team." And followed that with, "Well, I know what you are going to say, I must be in a hell of a shape if these are five of the finest individuals."

But they really were. Welton is so well-respected today. Nall and Hudson from the offensive line. Ros, Woerner. You had a pretty good group of people.

But I quickly caught myself, and I told him, "Let me assure you that if you will let me handle this, these young men will learn their lesson."

A Lesson in Leadership

Frank Ros said he learned lessons in leadership from both Erk Russell and me. And he said the way I handled the pig incident taught him a few things.

"He was ticked," Ros said. "He called us in, and you could tell he was angry. He was shocked.

"But I learned not to make an emotional decision. That is something to this day that I still do. You may be mad and you may be angry. Sleep on it for 24 hours and get the emotions out. He told us he was going to get to the bottom of this thing. In the meantime, we had to stay in the dorms. This was spring. Prime time. We sat in our rooms for two weeks."

The first meeting I had with them, when I called them into my office, I just laid into them about how embarrassing this was. I told them I was so mad that I didn't even want to talk to them, so I confined them to their rooms for a couple of days. They couldn't leave except to go to class.

Then a few days later they came back, and I told them what the punishment would be. I took them off scholarship. To earn their keep, they had to work, and part of that work was to paint the wall around the practice field during the hottest part of the day.

And I tried to scare them.

"Well, my first reaction is to just kick you all off the team," I said. "Besides, let me tell you how serious this is. These are experimental pigs that were injected with various types of serum. This particular one could be the one they were concerned about that might make you impotent."

I don't think all of them knew what that meant, but most of them did. I let them think about that for a few days. I put them through some hell, but they deserved it.

"Hugh and I walked out of there kind of chuckling," said Woerner, who I found out did not put much stock in the comment about possible impotence.

Welton said that the scariest thing for him was that look that I gave them in my office.

"I remember that look," he said. "Looking us up and down. That stare was the worst thing.

"The story I like to tell is this: I look around and next to me is Hugh Nall, our starting center; and Frank Ros, our team captain; Nat Hudson, All-SEC guard; and Scott Woerner, All-America cornerback, and I think we dodged that bullet. I'm thinking, 'What are you really going to do, Coach?' We had our scholarships taken away for the summer, and we had to work and paint that wall. So I learned that if you are going to do something bad, do it with guys who are pretty good."

Ros remembered it vividly.

"He calls us back in there. 'I've got a good mind to throw you all off the team.' In the end he told us, 'You all have to stay in summer school, you all have to attend classes, and you have to live in university housing and eat university food. You will work to pay restitution, and you will work out with Coach [John] Kasay.'

"The job was working with the athletics groundskeepers at first, working at the stadium. Then they decided to have us paint the walls on the perimeter of the practice field. Each field was 120 yards, the grass field and the AstroTurf. We had to paint it all summer long. The

1980 summer is still the record hot summer. There were 22 days it was over 100 degrees. You can look it up."

"It was the hottest summer on record," Woerner agreed. "We would go to class and after lunch work from 1:00 PM to 4:00 PM painting the wall and then work out with Coach Kasay and then go to night class," Ros said. "We did that the whole summer.

"Paint that cinderblock wall. It was hot and miserable. We got about 10 to 15 yards from the end. It was hotter than hell. In comes Coach Dooley in his Lincoln Town Car."

It sounds like a scene out of a grade B movie, a sinister fellow hidden behind a tinted window, revealed slowly as the electric window descends.

"He looks at us," Ros recalled, "and says, 'It ain't good enough. Do it again.' Here we go, just as we get to the end and start all over. Every bit of money we made, we never saw it; it went straight to restitution."

The five seniors spent countless hours together that summer, talking about the things that all young men talk about.

"We were trying to avoid Kasay," Woerner said. "We didn't have any place to hide. We didn't have any money."

Ros admitted that he violated one condition of his sentence. "Welton, Nall, and I got an apartment at Sussex," he said. "We had our room at the dorm, but we had residents looking out for us."

Welton's parents almost couldn't believe that he had been involved in this incident. He was in many ways the fair-haired child.

(Welton turned out to be a well-respected professional in sports marketing. He went to law school. He was with King & Spalding, one of the best law firms in the state. Then he worked with Billy Payne for the Olympics. Through that association he formed his own company to be the advertising agent for all of the Olympics. He sold that about the time I retired.

There were some who pushed Welton to be my successor as athletics director, and the search committee talked to him. He could have been a good one.)

David Davidson of the Atlanta paper broke the pig story first, getting a lot of his information from backup quarterback John Lastinger. I think Davidson kind of led on to Lastinger that he knew more than he did.

"Somebody tricked him pretty good," Ros laughed. "Of course, it is not that hard to trick a freshman. It got in the paper, and then in *Sports Illustrated* after that."

Needless to say, I was not too pleased with any of this.

A Rallying Point
When Defensive Coordinator Erk Russell looks back to the seeds of greatness for the 1980 team, he starts where many others start—with the quality of people on the team.

"We had some good people, and the attitude was good," he said, "but damn if I don't believe we built on the hog story."

There were many others who believed that the "purloined pig," as the headlines in the Atlanta newspaper called it, was a catalyst for team unity that could not have been manufactured.

"I wouldn't attribute our success to that incident," Chris Welton said, "but it was one of the factors. The five of us were all going to stay in the summer anyway. By having to work, a lot of the younger guys thought we had stepped up and taken responsibility."

"The five of us, we were the team leaders," Scott Woerner recalled. "We came back in the best shape of anybody on the team. It brought a lot of people together, mainly us. Everybody was close."

"I remember when Coach Russell was in the dining hall right after we got caught," Welton pointed out, "and he said, 'Chris, come over and eat with me.'

"And he said, 'Well, I understand we stole a pig.'"

"'Yes sir, we did.' The fact he used the term *we* stuck in my mind. We got in trouble, but everybody felt a part of the incident. Everybody felt responsible, but we took the fall. That caused people to appreciate us a little more, being responsible for what we did. That probably did have some carryover."

Erk knew I was tough on them for good reason.

"The rest of the team knew the origin of the pig and what happened," Erk said. "Hugh and Frank, all of them, were in positions of leadership on the team, and darn if I don't think it was a bond for everything.

"Now that may seem far-fetched to you, but it doesn't to me. Right off the bat, they had something in common. It drew the people together and the team, too."

"It brought the team together," Frank Ros said. "Coach Russell said he was glad it happened."

This summertime crisis could well have been part of the glue that brought this team together, perhaps more so than any team that I coached during my 25 years.

Rich Copley, *Athens Banner-Herald*

UGA V HAS ANIMAL MAGNETISM

One of the most enduring Georgia traditions is their mascot. From 1997
comes this story behind UGA the bulldog.

The annual University of Georgia football love fest is called Picture Day, but for these fans, it might as well be called UGA Day.

Several hundred Georgia faithful are slow-roasting under the late August afternoon sun just for a chance to get their picture snapped with UGA V, the solid-white English bulldog who is starting his eighth season patrolling the sidelines at UGA football games.

For those who get in—police have to cut off the line midway through the afternoon so UGA won't be overloaded—there's a chance to pet the pooch and maybe even receive a big, wet bulldog kiss.

The way Shawn Hutchinson, a junior from Warner Robins, Georgia, speaks of the two licks he got from UGA, you'd think Cindy Crawford had just given him a big smacker.

"I'll probably wash there after the season," he says of the spot on the right side of his face. "I've been watching Georgia football all of my life, and it's been a lifelong dream to meet UGA. I would have stood in a line a lot longer than this to meet UGA."

By the way, the line he stood in was about twice as long as the one for Bulldogs coach Jim Donnan. UGA's line made the crowds around players such as quarterback Mike Bobo and split end Hines Ward look like the crowd at the concession stand during a game-winning touchdown drive.

According to most of the fans, Picture Day goes a long way toward illustrating UGA's appeal—you and your children can and want to pet him.

"Most mascots you can't even get to," says Keith Bradford of McDonald, noting some of college football's lions, tigers, and bears. "Like South Carolina, the Gamecocks—nobody cares about an old chicken."

Bradford's three-year-old son, Brandon, had his picture taken with UGA. "To him, UGA is the University of Georgia," Bradford says.

During the afternoon, UGA is visited by kids dressed in Georgia football player and cheerleader uniforms, young men trying to look cool, and even UGA cheerleaders and members of the women's golf team.

And UGA-mania isn't reserved for Picture Day.

A Star Is Born

Before the Bulldogs' home opener against Arkansas State, the 49-pound Georgia mascot has trouble getting onto the field due to the crush of fans that surround him as he gets out of his red Ford Taurus with "UGA V" on the license plate. And throughout the game, he's besieged by camera-wielding fans leaning over the hedges, as well as newspaper and TV cameramen who visit his air-conditioned doghouse at the northeast corner of the Sanford Stadium field.

This devotion to the dog isn't new to the thousands of fans who flock to Athens on fall Saturday afternoons. But this year, the rest of the world is finding out about the greatest Bulldog of them all.

In April he appeared on the cover of *Sports Illustrated*'s "Jock Schools" issue with the designation, "No. 1 Mascot."

"If you can't appreciate the swaggering gait and Churchillian physiognomy of UGA V, the Bulldogs' bulldog, you must be a cat lover," the magazine wrote of the only guy in sports whose tongue hangs out more than Michael Jordan's.

With sports lovers clued in, Hollywood is next, as UGA will appear in Clint Eastwood's big-screen adaptation of John Berendt's best-seller *Midnight in the Garden of Good and Evil*. The move is scheduled to open December 25.

UGA's appearance on the *SI* cover and in the blockbuster-to-be, as well as other achievements, will be recognized at today's game, where a tribute to the bulldog will take place between the national anthem and the players' taking the field.

Long Line of UGAs

When the Bulldog faithful talk about UGA, they use the word *tradition* so much you'd think he'd been around as long as the Arch, which was erected in 1864.

But the UGA line is actually 91 years younger than the North Campus fixture.

When Cecelia Seiler received UGA I as a gift in 1955, she had no idea what she was getting into.

She and her husband, Frank W. "Sonny" Seiler, were students at the university, and Cecelia was only vaguely familiar with Mike, the bulldog who had served as the Georgia mascot from 1951 to his death in 1955.

With Mike's death, the school needed a new mascot, and former tennis coach Dan Magill suggested that UGA—then named Hood's Ole Dan—would be an ideal choice.

Before UGA, Georgia was represented officially by two bulldogs, Mike and his predecessor, Butch, who served from 1947 to 1950. Previous Georgia mascots included a goat in 1892 and a female bull terrier in 1894.

UGA started his duties as mascot in 1956, and "the students reacted positively to him right away," Cecelia Seiler remembers. "We went back to every game because UGA appealed to them. This was a dog they could relate to."

The UGA line was assured of its place in Georgia football when Savannah lawyer and then–state representative Alan Gaynor introduced a resolution in the Georgia state legislature that said all University of Georgia mascots would be descendants of UGA.

UGA I was on the sidelines through 1965. In 1966, UGA II took over and reigned until 1972. UGA III was on hand for Georgia's finest hour, the Bulldogs' national championship victory at the Sugar Bowl in 1981.

UGA IV became the mascot at the 1981 season opener against Tennessee and proceeded to go to a bowl game every year of his reign, which ran through the 1989 season. He was also on hand when Herschel Walker was awarded the Heisman Trophy in 1982 and was the only UGA to be hurt during a season. Charles Seiler, the Seilers' son who has handled UGA on the sidelines for most games since he was 13, says UGA IV injured himself in a fall. At a few games, he wore a white jersey with a red cross on it like injured players wear, while his brother, Otto, filled in as the mascot.

UGA V became the mascot in 1990. All of his predecessors are buried in vaults near the south entrance to the stadium.

One of UGA V's most notable moments came at last year's Auburn game, when he confronted Auburn running back Robert Baker after he scored a touchdown. While it seemed like a great example of the dog striking out against the enemy, Charles Seiler says it could have just as easily been a Georgia player he went after.

"Bulldogs just go after fast-moving things," he says.

Having a Good Time

It helps that UGA V is one of the most playful UGAs, Seiler says, shortly after a short game of tag on the sideline.

Seiler has to coax UGA to turn around and look at fans who want to take his picture because UGA likes to watch the game. But on this afternoon, with the temperatures in the high 90s, the bulldog often retreats to his air-conditioned doghouse where he chews on ice cubes.

As the season progresses and temperatures get cooler, Seiler says UGA gets more playful.

"If we can get through the first game of the year, we're fine," he says. The biggest distraction of the game for UGA comes in the third quarter when UGA spots Sonny Seiler rounding the southeast corner of the field. Suddenly he pulls his red leash taught lurching forward in an effort to meet his master.

The elder Seiler plays a little game of hide-and-seek with UGA, standing behind the pad wrapped around the east goal post so UGA can't see him. "Where'd he go?" is written all over the dog's face.

Most fans' passion for UGA is likely exceeded by Sonny Seiler's passion for Georgia football.

"He scoffs at any of our children who say they have something else to do on the day of a Georgia football game," Cecelia Seiler says. "Georgia football and our church are the two most important things to him."

The Seilers' arrangement is essentially that they own the dog and the University of Georgia owns the name. The family doesn't get financial compensation for bringing UGA to games or other events such as Bulldog Club meetings. The Seilers get two sideline passes for each game for UGA's handlers. And any money generated by UGA's name or image goes back to the university.

"It's really a perfect arrangement for both of us," Cecelia Seiler says. "They don't have to be bothered with caring for the dog, and we don't have to endure any of the financial burden of the paperwork or taxes."

Because UGA's name is copyrighted, it can't be used in advertising any of his offspring for sale.

"It will say UGA on the dog's papers," Cecelia Seiler says. "But they can't advertise it."

That said, UGA has been a ticket to some pretty prestigious places, such as the floor of the U.S. House of Representatives, where he was invited by Speaker Newt Gingrich.

Whatever public functions UGA attends, they are approved by the University of Georgia Athletic Department. That's not a demand the university has made, but more a courtesy the Seilers extend to UGA.

"I think they get tired of hearing all of the stuff UGA does," Cecilia Seiler says.

Among the things the school approved was UGA's appearance in *Midnight* and the *Sports Illustrated* shoot, which Seiler did not know would result in the cover of the magazine until it came out.

"People started calling me and saying, 'Have you seen the cover, have you seen the cover?'" she recalls. "I went out to get a copy, but they were already sold out. It took us about a week to get a copy."

The movie crew included two animal trainers, and there was another dog set to substitute for UGA if he proved camera shy. But he didn't.

UGA, who is a character in the movie because Sonny Seiler was one of the attorneys in the real-life Savannah murder trial the book is based on, dutifully walked through take after take, primarily guided by actor John Cusack, Cecelia Seiler says.

She recalls one scene in particular in which UGA was sitting in Sonny Seiler's Savannah office and Eastwood crouched behind the camera to direct him. Eastwood let out a soft bark to UGA, and UGA barked right back, impressing the Academy Award–winning director.

Sonny Seiler also appears in the movie as the judge and has a role in *The Gingerbread Man*, which was shot in Savannah and is scheduled for release in October.

But the Georgia fans don't need to worry that their proud pooch and his owners have gone Hollywood. Though he's not Georgia's longest-running tradition, plans are for UGA to continue to be one of the university's most enduring.

"A lot of things change," Charles Seiler says, walking out of Sanford Stadium with UGA after the season opener ends. "But there's always going to be a white bulldog here, and you can count on that."

NOTES

The publisher has made every effort to determine the copyright holder for each piece in *Echoes of Georgia Football*.

Reprinted courtesy of *The Sporting News*: "More Than a Passing Grade" by Dave Kindred, copyright © August 29, 1994. Reprinted with permission.

Reprinted courtesy of *The Atlanta Journal-Constitution*: "Sports of Winter," copyright © 1892 by *The Atlanta Journal-Constitution* (GA) in the format Other Book via Copyright Clearance Center; "Bob M'Whorter" by Dick Jemison, copyright © 1913 by *The Atlanta Journal-Constitution* (GA) in the format Other Book via Copyright Clearance Center.

Reprinted courtesy of *The New York Times*: "Georgia Defeats Texas Christian" by Louis Effrat, copyright © 1942 by The New York Times Co. Reprinted with permission; "Man in the Right Place for Georgia," copyright © 1983 by The New York Times Co. Reprinted with permission; "Yale Beaten, 15–10, by Georgia 11 in a Stirring Game" by Robert F. Kelley, copyright © 1929 by The New York Times Co. Reprinted with permission.

Reprinted courtesy of *The New York Times Magazine*: "Herschel Walker's Run to Glory" by Henry Liefermann, copyright © 1981 by The New York Times Co. Reprinted with permission.

Reprinted courtesy of the *Washington Post*: "Bowl Trips Are Annual Affairs for Georgia" by Morris Siegel, copyright © 1948 by the *Washington Post*. Reprinted with permission; "Dooley: Man in Need of a Fitting Image" by Gary Pomerantz, copyright © 1982 by the *Washington Post*. Reprinted with permission.

Reprinted courtesy of Alex Crevar: "Kicking Down the Door" by Alex Crevar, copyright © 2002 by Alex Crevar. Reprinted with permission.